CONTENTS

GW00482904

Contents

How to use this book

The *Beginner's Guide* series aims to introduce readers to major writers of the past 500 years. It is assumed that readers will begin with little or no knowledge and will want to go on to explore the subject in other ways.

BEGIN READING THE AUTHOR

This book is a companion guide to Morrison's major works, it is not a substitute for reading the books themselves. It would be useful if you read some of the works in parallel, so that you can put theory into practice. This book is divided into sections. After considering how to approach the author's work and a brief biography, we go on to explore some of Morrison's main writings and themes before examining some critical approaches to the author. The survey finishes with suggestions for further reading and possible areas of further study.

HOW TO APPROACH UNFAMILIAR OR DIFFICULT TEXTS

Coming across a new writer may seem daunting, but do not be put off. The trick is to persevere. Much good writing is multi-layered and complex. It is precisely this diversity and complexity which makes literature rewarding and exhilarating.

Literary work often needs to be read more than once and in different ways. These ways can include: a leisurely and superficial reading to get the main ideas and narrative; a slower more detailed reading focusing on the nuances of the text and on what appear to be key passages; and reading in a random way, moving back and forth through the text to examine different aspects, such as themes, narrative or characterization.

In complex texts it may be necessary to read in short chunks. When it comes to tackling difficult words or concepts it is often enough to guess in context on the first reading, making a more detailed study using a dictionary or book of critical concepts on later reading. If you prefer to look up unusual words as you go along, be careful that you do not disrupt the flow of the text and your concentration.

VOCABULARY

You will see that keywords and unfamiliar terms are set in **bold** text. These words are also defined and explained in the glossary to be found at the back of the book.

This book is a tool to help you appreciate a key figure in literature. We hope you enjoy reading it and find it useful.

✴ ✴ ✴ *SUMMARY* ✴ ✴ ✴

To maximize the use of this book:

- read the author's work;

- read it several times in different ways;

- be open to innovative or unusual forms of writing;

- persevere.

Why Read Toni Morrison?

A WONDERFUL STORYTELLER

Toni Morrison is a spellbinding weaver of stories which mix both the historical real and the magical, supernatural and the imaginative in people's lives. As a key African-American woman writer, Toni Morrison has rewritten and revitalized a history which largely ignored African-Americans and women in particular. Her work is energetic and lively; it is beautifully, lyrically and dramatically written, and engages the reader in compelling issues about equality, and racial and sexual politics. It is also immensely entertaining, tragic, ironic, amusing, and enriched with fascinating details of people's lives. Toni Morrison is a significant figure in contemporary writing, in women's writing and in African-American writing. Her stories are gripping, emotional, drawn from both a literary and an oral tradition; they appeal to a wide and international readership.

We read Toni Morrison for several reasons. One is that she tells wonderful stories, bringing to life the lived experiences of African-American women and men from different periods in time, creating a sense of the different communities in which they live, and their different histories. For example, in *Sula* we want to know more about Sula, a disturbing influence in the lives of those around her in the all-**Black** township in which she lives. In *Beloved*, we want to know about the legacy of slavery and how Sethe can establish a sense of identity in the face of such abuse. In *Jazz* we want to know not 'who done it' with the murder of young Dorcas, but why such a

KEYWORD

Black: the use of Black as a proper noun indicates the recognition of and identification with race, with being Black. It is a seizing of identity which emerged during the Civil Rights Movement, and has been embraced particularly by Black feminists and others.

murder was a seemingly inevitable result for Dorcas and her lover; we want to know about the lies and pressures on African-American lives in Harlem in the Jazz Age. We care about the individuals who come to life for us on Morrison's pages.

AFRICAN-AMERICAN HISTORY REDISCOVERED

We also want to know about the periods of African-American history which Toni Morrison recuperates from absence. Toni Morrison found no mention of Black people in crucial moments in our shared history and no mention of the moments which were crucial specifically to the history of African-Americans, from their viewpoint. Through her research, she brings to life these periods and moments as felt experiences, telling us stories about the people of those times, which include the period of the late days of slavery, World War II, the 1960s and the Jazz Age. We also read Toni Morrison because she focuses on women's lives. In *The Bluest Eye, Song of Solomon* and *Jazz*, she looks at the destructive influence of a (white-defined) cosmeticized beauty for young Black girls and women. This encourages them to buy into a materialistic culture which actually has little place for their own versions of beauty, because it values white beauty above that of Black.

Toni Morrison uses imagery, symbols and metaphors as motifs which run throughout her work. These are concrete, real things, such as cosmetics and fancy shoes in *Jazz* which represent materialism, or a bag full of what is thought to be gold but turns out to be ancestral bones, in *Song of Solomon*. She actually uses real things to act as symbols of relationships, behaviours, attitudes and trends. She is a wonderful storyteller in the oral storytelling model, turned into published format. Morrison fascinates her readers with the lives of individuals, with rich evocations of specific periods, and with the telling of events, their implications and effects.

She has a design on us and messages to pass on concerned with individuals and the community, the importance of specifically African-American people whose lives have largely been ignored. She invites us into the lives of individuals and explores the ways in which communities treat people. One example is in the witch hunts for the powerful women in *Paradise*. Another is in *Sula* when the community constructs Sula as a pariah – Sula actually acts as a scapegoat for their own bad ways; blaming her offloads their own guilt. Some of the messages are about the importance of individuals, others about heritage, memory, myth, beauty and self-worth. Some have key messages about the importance of recuperating the lived real past of individual African-Americans, of African-American people and of people more generally.

Toni Morrison is a Nobel prize winner and major voice in Black writing. Her works present many voices and versions which place the reader at the centre, probably of a community, able to measure versions, experiences, perceptions and representations. Morrison's work is essentially **dialogic**, that is, it presents arguments about individual values, experiences, periods and readings of events. Morrison invites the reader to engage in a dialogue with these versions even as it places us in the centre of a community who also engage in such dialogue between different versions of history and reality. She suggests we can make meaning, rather than having a single meaning imposed upon us. Rigid, single interpretations and sets of values can cause rejection of difference, which can lead to racism and

> **KEYWORD**
>
> Dialogic: coined first by Russian critic Mikhail Bakhtin (1895–1975), dialogic suggests a dialogue, debate or argument between ideas and points of view. Typically an author might show different views of different people, or different interpretations and representations in different times and places. Together they form a debate suggesting there are no single right answers or interpretations – so none should be forced on people or events.

sexism. Those who mistakenly believe they have the single right way of behaving can impose this upon others, disempowering and dehumanizing them in the process. By recreating dialogue, through different voices, irony, imagery and so on, in her work, she invites us into the debates, and engages us in the issues.

Morrison sets up debates and discussions, versions showing how different people construct reality, make different interpretations. The dialogic form fits well with an oral storytelling form. Like a debate, it enables readers to see that form, and to see that people construct meanings, histories, value and interpretations that *could* actually be different from those passed on as the right ones. This opens up readers' views. We can see how different people felt and thought at different times, and we can start to question what we might otherwise take for granted, such as practices and beliefs about good and evil, men and women, Black and white.

MAGIC AND HISTORY

One major trend in African-American women's writing is that of mixing magic and history. History provides the opportunity for testimony and a record of the uncharted times and lives of Black people ever present but virtually invisible in social and literary terms until they started to be written of – mostly in the 1970s onwards. Toni Morrison's fine blend of the magical, supernatural, spiritual, imaginative and metaphorical with the historical and realistic has caused some criticism among those who would seek to limit Black women's writing to testimony and record alone. This kind of restraint upon form and language is yet another covert example of racism that seeks to subordinate others' voices and expression.

Her engaged aim is a full record which recreates and revitalizes history through factual testimony and a recreation of the imaginative world.

* * *SUMMARY* * *

We read Morrison's work because it has:

- fascinating stories about individuals whose lives interest us;

- a profound sense of history which is recreated, rewritten, rediscovered in front of us and which places hidden, silenced African-American people at its centre;

- insights into the individual lives of people, their hopes and fears and experiences such as that of slavery (*Beloved*), of living in the Jazz Age (*Jazz*);

- beautiful, lyrical use of language combining the historically real, and the magical or supernatural;

- a sense of debate and dialogue which enables us to see how people construct versions, values and meanings;

- a real sense of the total engagement with issues that matter, such as equality across ethnic, gendered and class/social boundaries.

2 How to Approach Toni Morrison's Work

Writing is about danger for me; it's like life – you can go under.
(Interview with Stuart in McKay, Nellie, *Critical essays on Toni Morrison*, Boston, GK Hall, 1988)

A Nobel prize winner and major voice in Black writing, Toni Morrison said she set out to write the novels which she wanted to read, but couldn't find – novels about the joys and pains of everyday life for African-American people, at different points in history. Her writing is poetic, beautiful, lively, both magical and realistic at the same time. Morrison rediscovers and recuperates periods in African-American history emphasizing both the hardships and inequalities experienced by African-Americans, and celebrating their energies, creativity, community spirit and individuality. Her work brings to light the lives of ordinary, varied, individual Black people, particularly women, who have suffered under slavery, moved to the northern cities such as New York to find work and a new life, or settled on the outskirts of towns and experienced economic hardships.

I think that all good art has always been political. None of the best writing, the best thoughts have been anything other than that.
(Interview with Alice Childress, 1994)

In reading Morrison's work and that of other African-American writers, and indeed of other writers whose cultural and historical background might differ from our own, it is essential that we know something about the historical and aesthetic context of that work. We should not merely read it as if it is a product of our own context and like every other book we have read. This is particularly the case with Black writing and Black women's writing because much of it, and Toni Morrison's work in particular, deliberately sets out to relate to and to relate (tell about) a history which has been hidden because of prejudice springing from racial difference. Assuming we can read such work without knowledge of the context of her aims, we could possibly (and unintentionally) just be making assumptions, misreading, appropriating this work, taking it over and assimilating it, joining it in seamlessly, with **the canon**. History and culture inform Morrison's own views and those of Black women's criticism can also inform our reading. This should not silence us, but we do need to understand context and critical perspectives.

> **KEYWORD**
>
> The Canon: a term used to suggest the most important, most frequently read and taught literature. It includes Shakespeare and Wordsworth, but is largely a white, male middle-class group of writers. It has often excluded women and Black writers.

SOURCES: ORAL STORYTELLING

Morrison's work springs in part from oral storytelling, or folk art; it uses repeated motifs, circularity and different versions, and produces the sounds and voices of the people. Much of her writing is based upon musical forms, and reminds us of the motifs, the energies of music. *Jazz* focuses on the Jazz Age and forms of jazz, *Beloved* on the blues. Many voices in her novels place us, the reader, at the centre of a community. She concentrates on how, at different historical moments in different contexts, people's lives have been represented, or ignored. Toni Morrison values the influence and power of her heritage, recuperating historical, lived moments in African-American history to fill in the blanks, give voice to voiceless people hidden largely from official history. Her work also deals with gendered relations, women's lives, motherhood, sisterhood, the community and sexual politics.

In her writing, Toni Morrison blends the magical, mystical, supernatural and spiritual with historical realism because each captures different elements of our lives. She combines metaphor and image with historical dates and details. In *Beloved*, she uses newspaper reports as jumping-off points to investigate how the horrific inhumanities of slavery could cause a sensitive woman (Margaret

Garner in real life, Sethe in the novel) to decide her children were better off dead than enslaved. In *Jazz*, she explores the largely ignored murder of a young Black woman by an infatuated cosmetic salesman. This incident represents how, in the Jazz Age, the **American Dream** promised all sorts of lively possibilities in New York but really sold Black people out.

She achieves something unforgettable, vital, new, a real testimony to the lived history of people's lives – both what they do and what they feel and dream. It is writing which makes us think, care about people's lives, become involved, and marvel at the beauty of the language and images she uses to capture and maintain our interest.

Speaking out against history that silences you and establishing the worth of your own identity is a major issue in Black women's writing. By exploring different individuals as part of different communities in all their variety, at different points in history, Toni Morrison can fill in everyone's knowledge and understanding of, and appreciation and empathy with the diverse lives of African-Americans. These insights can also lead us to explore and appreciate writing by writers from other cultural contexts, making us somewhat more aware of the need to find out about these contexts in terms of what they record, how people experienced and perceived their lives, and the different forms of expression available in different cultures.

> **KEYWORD**
>
> American Dream: the idea of the American Dream, derives from the pioneering frontier spirit which drove people to America hoping to seek their fortunes and their futures. It suggests that America can reward and celebrate people for their endeavours, and that it is a great, generous country. Many found that this was not the reality they actually met, encountering instead hardships, everyday difficulties and dis-illusionment. Many writers, including F. Scott Fitzgerald (1896–1940) who wrote *The Great Gatsby* (1925) have shown that the Dream was a deception.

READING *BELOVED*

Beloved (1987) is a novel about the legacy of the horrific past of slavery. It is partly a ghost story of a baby who returns, grown up, to haunt the mother who caused her death. It is much more than this, however.

Beloved (now a major film, 1999) directly confronts racism in a novel that combines lyrical beauty with an assault on the reader's emotions and conscience. It traces, embodies and focuses on the legacy of slavery, using forms – oral storytelling and metaphor – derived from a traditional Black folk aesthetic. Both content and form are controversial, difficult, but immensely rewarding and thought-provoking for the reader or teacher/student. The novel makes us aware of the dehumanizing horror of slavery, and is essentially about the vitality and intrusiveness of memory, the memory of racial oppression under slavery. History is a tangible, visible existent that a community can experience, bump into. The end of the novel celebrates the ability of people to live on, to cope with painful histories and memories and find a new, energetic, self-aware sense of identity. The ability to face up to the memories of racism and establish a new set of relationships, a new sense of self-worth is ultimately empowering for African-Americans, for whites, and for Sethe herself. She learns, as Paul D., her lover, points out, 'You your own best thing, Sethe.' (p. 273)

A close look at the opening

The novel opens with some rather confusing statements: '124 was spiteful, full of a baby's venom'(p. 3). This surprises the reader because there has been no scene setting, no introduction to character, period, theme as you would find in a traditional nineteenth-century novel. Some historical detail does follow, however, and we are told that Cincinnati, Ohio is where the tale is set and at one point in history (the period of the establishment of the community, when the Northern American States started to let ex-slaves live as free people) there had been no street numbers.

Time

The time in which the tale is set moves around. There is a mention of (1) 'Now', the contemporary late-twentieth century, to help us locate our own responses, as readers, and Toni Morrison's responses as a creative re-creator of a historical period; (2) of a period when there were street numbers – the house we are focusing on is number 124 (3) a period previous to that when there were no street numbers because the community was just becoming established.

These time periods are important in the novel. The most historically distant period (4) is one in which Sethe and her family undergo their experiences as slaves on the farmstead 'Sweet Home' (short for 'Home sweet home') where initially the owner, Mr Garner, allows Sethe and Halle to marry and produce children. This was unusually tolerant in a period in which slaves were kept segregated by gender and not allowed to live together in families. In this historically distant period the farm was taken over by a tyrannical but learned man, Schoolteacher, who taught white children to differentiate between Black slaves and themselves, as if the Black people were closer to animals then humans. This education into racism leads to Sethe's sufferings and whippings, and to the destruction of all the Black male slaves who either escape, go mad or are burned – all save Paul D., who seeks Sethe out in Cincinnati. Sethe and her children escape across the river into new freedom, living with Baby Suggs, Halle's mother, a community leader skilled in midwifery and herbalism. But Schoolteacher and his men, including the slave-catcher, cross the river too, coming to take them back for punishment, and into slavery. Faced with the prospect of a life of abuse and dehumanization for herself and her children, Sethe attempts to kill them, which in her desperate state she sees as a form of rescue. The baby dies.

Period (2) is the period of the main focus of the events of the novel, when Sethe's dead baby returns, a fully grown woman, and lives in the family with Sethe, Paul D. and Denver, her own sister.

Magic and history

Returning to the first sentence, 'full of a baby's venom' is surprising as babies are not usually considered venomous. This one, however, is a revengeful ghostly presence, who causes strange supernatural events rather like a poltergeist might in a haunted house. 124 is exactly that, a haunted house. The baby ghost leaves handprints in the food, shapes in the mirror, causes spillages and alarm among the whole family in the house. She is a very real presence and this presence has, we are told, frightened away both the young men, her brothers, Howard and Buglar. Toni Morrison here creates a historical reality – the dates, places, the event of a real death of a real child at her own mother's protective hands – and presents the reader with the lived reality of a ghost, using the same tones to describe the supernatural as she does to record the historical. In this way she mixes the magical and the historical to emphasize how our lives are a mixture of the factual and our feelings, myths, and imaginative realities. By setting the tale in several moments in the history of slavery and involving the reader in interpreting the mixture of historical fact and revived memory, she suggests that the memory of slavery is part of all our heritage. It has to be faced up to, managed and lived through. People must not forget its horrors, and they must live with them daily (as Sethe does the lived presence of her dead baby, a full grown ghostly presence felt as real) but they need to move on, also.

The baby ghost's handprints scared away her brothers.

Toni Morrison uses real events in history on which to base her tale. Margaret Garner (as reported in the local newspapers) escaped with her children across the river to Ohio, and killed one child in an attempt to prevent them all from being recaptured when the slave-catcher came in 1855 to force her back into slavery. By focusing on this true historical event and exploring the way in which people might have responded and reacted, Toni Morrison brings hidden parts of history to life. She also enables readers to empathize with people whose lives they could not otherwise fully imagine. In the case of *Beloved*, she confronts the guilty history of racial oppression as it manifests itself in the intolerable practice of slavery, a dehumanizing experience which causes dehumanizing acts in others.

Storytelling

These opening sentences also involve us in wanting to find out about the family, who the venomous baby is, who the grandmother Baby Suggs is, what her community power is or has been, and why the two brothers left. We want to know about these people as individuals and about the periods into which Toni Morrison is taking us. Unravelling the history and becoming bound up in the fascinating story of these people's lives is begun for the reader in the first couple of pages of the novel. We are also made aware that there will be some traumatic events disclosed – enough to frighten family members away. The tone is documentary and spellbinding.

The slave-catcher incident

The arrival of the slave-catcher (near the middle of the book, p.148) to recapture Sethe and her children and return them to an abusive life under slavery is the novel's most terrifying and powerful moment. It is deliberately placed near the middle of the book. This is important because we have by then grown to understand and love Sethe in her struggles to bring up her children, in her terrible memories of abuse under slavery, the deaths of her husband and the other men on the plantation, and her responses to the arrival of Beloved, a young woman believed to be her dead baby, now fully grown. Our sympathies for Sethe enable us to understand why she acts as she does and to appreciate that the return of the dead baby as a ghostly, lived presence is the result of the shocking practice of slavery and the response it causes in others. For Black and white alike, slavery is a memory deeply embedded in all our histories, returning and dominating our thoughts, perhaps preventing us from moving on in relations between Black and white, faced with the anger, or the guilt we feel.

The novel dramatizes this key incident of the arrival of the slave-catcher. The incident starts apocalyptically: 'When the four horsemen came' (p.148). This is a reference to the four horsemen of the Apocalypse, whose terrible arrival heralds the end of the world in the Bible (Revelations). Toni Morrison uses language very carefully and precisely, placing us as readers inside the head of the slave-catcher at one moment, Schoolteacher at another. We are experiencing their shared views from the inside and so appreciating how monstrous their interpretation of events is. The fugitive slaves are described as if they are children playing guilty games. Dehumanized, they are also described as wild animals:

> Caught red-handed, so to speak, they would seem to recognize the futility of outsmarting a white man and the hopelessness of outrunning a rifle. Smile even, like a child caught dead with his hand in the jelly jar, and when you reached for the rope to tie him, well, even then you couldn't tell. The very nigger with his head hanging and a little jelly-jar smile on his face could all of a sudden roar, like a bull or some such, and commence to do disbelievable things...
>
> (*Beloved*, p.148)

We are brought into the scene, made inclusive, because he speaks to us as insiders. We are given lessons and rules about how to ensure that the slaves are not turned wild in the first place (by over beating like a dog or a horse) and how to recapture them carefully so that they are not harmed (this reduces their worth). Slaves, distanced and made **Other** than us, are called 'they' or even 'it' and are considered valuable only as property, of less use than an animal when dead: 'Unlike a snake or a bear, a dead nigger could not be skinned for profit and was not worth his own dead weight in coin' (p.148).

> **KEYWORD**
>
> Other: to make someone else 'Other' is to identify all that is strange and unpleasant and to blame it on someone else, to turn them into something which is not yourself, which is strange. 'Otherizing' people is an element of racism and sexism.

The tone of collusion is sickening, and the mindset, or viewpoint into which we are placed, is brutal, abusive. The reader has inside knowledge, a first-hand, first-person narrative view of someone who treats people as less than animals and feels he is in the right to do so. Such inside knowledge enables us both to appreciate why Sethe tries to kill her children, and to sympathize totally with her as an individual. It enables us to imagine more clearly the all too common horrors of slavery, as if we were on the scene, rather than through the distant sense of a history book. It also enables us to appreciate much more clearly the warping effects of slavery on the minds of those who perpetuate it.

In the face of such 'humanity', the 'crazy' mother, Sethe, murders her child to save her. It is a stark, terrible description:

> Inside, two boys bled in the sawdust and dirt at the feet of a nigger woman holding a blood-soaked child to her chest and an infant by the heels in the other. She did not look at them; she simply swung the baby toward the wall planks, missed and tried to connect a second time.
>
> (*Beloved*, p.149)

The 'pickaninnies' are now considered worthless, and Sethe's anguished act just a product of the nephew's 'mishandling' of her, as one might mishandle a dog: 'Suppose you beat the hounds past that point that away. Never again could you trust them in the woods or anywhere else' (p.149).

The novel provides such vivid insights into the lived experience of slavery and its legacy that it has had a very powerful effect on readers and as a film on audiences. It explores how people's minds at the times of slavery and ever since can be haunted by the horrors of slavery, haunted as if by a lived presence of a ghost returning, repressed, difficult to live with, difficult to speak about and difficult to ignore. So the novel teaches us and enlightens us by bringing such experiences to life.

* * *SUMMARY* * *

Morrison's work:

• establishes a great voice in African-American women's writing, concerned with writing about Black people, for all readers;

• combines realism, history with magic, the supernatural to recuperate past, hidden histories and people's imaginative lives;

• asserts importance of identity, speaking out against racism, sexism and silencing;

• explores everyday texture of people's lives, emphasizing the lives of victims, and strong, imaginative, energetic women and men;

• uses musical references, forms and expressions;

• uses oral storytelling, myth and legend to give a sense of community and history.

3 Biography and Influences

PERSONAL

Toni Morrison was born in Lorain, Ohio, on 18 February 1931 as Chloe Anthony Wofford; she later changed her name. Toni was the second of four children and her parents, George and Ramah Wofford, were working class, from Southern families. Her grandparents on her mother's side had moved to Lorain from Alabama via Kentucky where her grandfather worked as a coalminer, and her father, George, came to Ohio to escape the racial violence he experienced in Georgia, his home. For many years her father held down three jobs at the same time. In the Depression he suffered alongside others in Lorain, a town on Lake Erie in which people worked in steel mills and shipyards. He only recovered financially in 1949. In Lorain many Black migrants sought work when their roles as **sharecroppers** disappeared and they lost their land.

> **KEYWORD**
>
> Sharecropping: when slavery was abolished in North America in 1865 many people became sharecroppers, working with the crops on a plantation for a share of those crops or the price they produced when sold. It was a hard life and a poor living.

In 1953, Toni Morrison gained a BA in English from Howard University and in 1955 an MA from Cornell University, where she wrote her thesis on William Faulkner, the white Southern American writer (1897–1962). In 1958, she married Harold Morrison, a Jamaican architect and had two sons, Harold Ford and Slade Kevin. Toni and Harold Morrison were divorced in 1964.

CAREER

Toni Morrison has had a distinguished career as a teacher, editor and professor. From 1955–57 she was an English teacher at Texas Southern

University, Houston, returning to Howard University in 1957 for seven years. Following this period of teaching she turned to publishing and became a senior editor at the New York publishing company, Random House, where she worked from 1965–85. From 1971–72, Morrison was Associate Professor of English at the State University of New York, in Purchase, and from 1984–89, she held the Albert Schweitzer Chair in the Humanities at the State University of New York in Albany. Since 1989, Morrison has been the Robert F. Goheen Professor in the Council of the Humanities at Princeton University, New Jersey.

Alongside her teaching and publishing, Morrison began to write. A single working mother, she found it difficult juggling writing novels, working as an editor at Random House and raising her children but found (like other women writers such as Sylvia Plath and Elizabeth Gaskell) that she could write first thing in the morning.

HER NOVELS

Toni Morrison's first book *The Bluest Eye* (1969) deals with the abusive life suffered by a young African-American girl, Pecola Breedlove. Pecola, internalizing cultural values which make her feel silenced, ugly and second rate because of her colour, suffers rape, the loss of her baby, and a real loss of identity and sanity. This novel made a strong powerful statement about the dehumanization of Black people under racism. It was followed by *Sula* (1973), which won a National Book Award Nomination and the Ohioana Book Award (1975). *Sula* also focuses on growing up in a Black town, on friendship, the nature of evil and the constraints upon Black people's lives. *Song of Solomon* (1977), which looks at identity and history, achieved the National Book Critics Circle Award and the American Academy and Institute of Arts and Letters Award (1977). *Tar Baby* (1981) deals with Jadine and Son's search for identity, and their outcast status. It was followed in 1986 by the play *Dreaming Emmett* which told the tale of 14-year-old Emmett Till, a young Black boy lynched in Mississippi. *Beloved* (1987) is a powerful and disturbing novel which mixes history and the supernatural. It draws from the life of a real person, Margaret Garner, named Sethe in the novel, who flees from slavery with her young family into Ohio, only to be hunted down by slave-catchers. Faced with the horror of recapture and abuse, she chooses to murder her own baby, who then returns as a ghostly, lived presence. Morrison received the New York State Governor's Arts Award, and a nomination for the National Book Critics Circle Award for this novel, which was the first to receive the Washington College Literary Award. *Beloved* also won the Pulitzer Prize for Fiction, the Robert F. Kennedy award and the Elizabeth Cady Stanton Award from the National Organization for Women in 1988. In 1993, *Beloved* won the Nobel prize for Literature. *Beloved* was followed by *Jazz* (1992), *Playing in the Dark: Whiteness and the Literary Imagination* (1992) and *Paradise* (1998).

Morrison's novels focus on the African-American community, and are typically set in towns resembling her birthplace, a crossing point between North and South, neither plantation nor ghetto. Her novels focus on the unique cultural inheritance of African-Americans through the complexities of ethical issues, memory and inter-personal relationships, and searchingly explore the African-American family and codes of femininity. *The Bluest Eye* and *Sula* consider in different ways the traumatic process of growing up as an African-American woman. In *Song of Solomon* friendship and memory, and the recovery of family and community history through folklore are interwoven in the story of 'Milkman Dead'.

SOCIAL, POLITICAL AND CULTURAL BACKGROUND

African-American slavery has been widely written about. For example, W.E Dubois in his *Black Reconstruction in America 1860–1880* (1935) saw slavery as not always deliberately cruel, when compared with the suffering after freedom and work noted by Eugene D. Genovese in *Roll Jordon Roll: The World, The Slave Trade* (1974). Visitors to the slave museums of Hull and Liverpool in the UK will find documented and visual evidence of the cruelty of selling and transporting people, from different tribes in different parts of Africa, in exchange for cash and goods. Those who survived the cramped insanitary conditions of the long crossing to America could be treated often worse than animals while working as slaves on American plantations. Those who profited by this enslavement and transportation included unscrupulous African chiefs, plantation owners and British capitalists whose profits helped build the great Victorian cities of England such as Liverpool, Manchester and Bristol. Separated from partners, their families sold away, women under slavery were, like the men, forced to work long hours in both the fields and domestic situations. Additionally, women were the subject of sexual abuse at the hands of white plantation owners and their managers. bell hooks' *Ain't I A Woman: Black Women and Feminism* (1981) provides thoroughly researched, horrific detail of this abuse which dehumanized women, casting them as various stereotypes, such as the Black whore (when they were forced into sexual relations with white men) and the Black Mammy. One element in the American Civil War (1861–65) was the Northern states' insistence that slaves be freed, while the Southern states, depending on slaves to work their plantations, disagreed. One result of the war was emancipation. For many slaves as freed people, what followed was the opportunity to seek paid work in the industrial north, while for others, lack of land ownership and any decent wage forced them into poverty, working as 'sharecroppers' – working the land for a small share of the crops produced. African-Americans had few legal rights and no right to the vote. Well documented also are the activities of the Civil Rights Movement of the mid-twentieth century when great thinkers and political figures such as Martin Luther King (1929–68) expressed their dreams of equality: 'I have a dream'.

One key stage in the development of a sense of identity crucial to all of us, and particularly so to people denied their identity, language and history, is to revisit and reclaim history. For African-American women writers this has been a central task as they research and re-imagine their forebears, their mothers and grandmothers. One central essay exploring the hidden creativity of Black women in the US is Alice Walker's *In Search of our Mother's Gardens* (1983) which focuses on the absence of Black women artists of all sorts, pointing out that their art was hampered by poverty, slavery and domestic drudgery. Walker puts forward the idea that much Black women's art did exist, but it was ephemeral, in the form of gardens, stitchwork and cooking.

AFRICAN-AMERICAN WOMEN WRITERS

African-American women writers concentrate on issues of race, colour, roots, motherhood, relationships, identity, women's roles and representations, community, the supernatural and the spiritual, recuperating and revivifying hidden histories. They are concerned with sexism as much as racism. Anne Petry, Gloria Naylor, Gwendolyn Brooks, Zora Neale Hurston, Nella Larson, Ntozake Shange and Maya Angelou are other well-known African-American women writers of fiction.

Early 1980s criticism of and by African-American women writers concentrated on recuperating the silenced writers of the past, and speaking out against racism and sexism. Issues of determining specific African-American women's language and expression were also central. A familiar theme was that of suffering and silencing, the 'triple burden' of which Zora Neale Hurston speaks in her novel *Their Eyes Were Watching God* (1937). Hurston's character Janey hears that the white man's burden is handed to the Black man, who hands it to the Black woman, designated under this triple burden of class, colour and gender, as 'the mule of the world'. A task for writers and critics alike was

KEY FACT

Martin Luther King (1929–68) was a key figure in the Civil Rights Movement. The movement was sparked off by a Black woman, Rosa Parkes, in Montgomery, Alabama. African-Americans were forced to sit at the back of the bus – an example of segregation. Rosa refused to do so and this led to the start of the actual Civil Rights Movement. After a year-long boycott of the buses, segregation was ruled illegal. During the riots, activism, lectures and inspirational writings and talks of the movement, King was assassinated (1968) as was the more radical Malcolm X (1965). A key woman figure on this period is the writer and activist Angela Davies, whose work inspired many women to seek both racial and gendered equality.

to rediscover hidden foremothers, both their own and their literary foremothers, in order to trace relationships and developments in African-American women's writing (Smith 1982; Greene and Kahn, 1985; Tate, 1985; Perry, 1976).

The necessity for this rediscovery, common in all women's critical writing of the 1970s and 1980s, has largely been superseded now by an interest in exploring the work of well-established women writers such as Alice Walker and Toni Morrison, considering the forms of a Black feminist criticism and the angles and discourse this might develop, and relating some of the concerns of African-American women, in their writing, with those of post-colonial women writers (Wisker, 1992; Wilentz, 1992).

Early history of African-American women writers

African-American women's writing has a relatively long history. Anne Lucy Terry, who wrote the poem 'Bars Fight' in 1746, was the first African-American woman to be published, and only the second woman published in America. She was followed by Phillis Wheatley, a slave, just nine when she arrived in America, who produced her first volume of poetry in 1773. In 1861 Harriet Jacobs authored *Incidents in the Life of a Slave Girl*, the first female slave narrative. This followed several Christian testimonies to the struggles of womanhood by free-born African-Americans, notably Jarena Lee and Zilpha Law. Jacobs' first-person slave narrative is a record of injustices experienced by women under slavery. The formal legacy of 'testifying' (personal experience) guarantees authenticity, encourages recognition of identity and has remained a feature of African-American women's writing.

The first novel was *Our Nig: Or Sketches for the Life of a Free Black* (1859) by Harriet E. Wilson. Latterly, contemporary writers such as Toni Morrison and Alice Walker, have featured in the syllabi of universities, colleges, adult classes and schools for several years. Literary activity has rescued silenced, disenfranchised and invisible Black women from the margins, enabling them to speak and to be seen and heard. Alice Walker's *The Color Purple* (1983), and the fictionalized autobiography sequence of Maya Angelou, which includes *I Know Why the Caged Bird Sings* (1970) grew from the earlier slave narratives and testimonies.

The major development period for Black writers was during the Jazz Age, in the 1930s, the period of the Harlem Renaissance when both Zora Neale Hurston and Nella Larsen wrote. Other prose writers of the period are Jessie Fauset and Dorothy West. Poets include Anne Spencer, Georgia Douglas Johnson, Gwendolyn Bennett and Helene Johnson.

When we look at the best-known contemporary African-American women writers such as Alice Walker, Toni Morrison and Maya Angelou, we find self-awareness, an educated and highly developed discourse and narrative style, integrated with a politicized engagement with issues of racism and sexism. Their asserted aim is to bring light to periods of history untold and hidden:

> I think my whole programme as a writer is to deal with history just so I know where I am.
>
> (Walker in *Tate*, 1985, p.185)

> ...to bear witness to a history that is unrecorded, untaught in mainstream education and to enlighten our people.
>
> (Morrison, 1985, p. 185)

Writing is seen as a historical act of reclamation, a way of recognizing and charting roots and identity. It is a political act of breaking silence for women from a diversity of backgrounds. Particularly notable is the deliberate development of expression which enables the articulation of experiences, thoughts, feelings and arguments unrecorded or marginalized in the discourse of male and particularly white male writers:

> The use of Black women's language and cultural experience in books by Black women ABOUT Black women results in a miraculously rich coalescing of form and content and also takes their writing far beyond the confines of white/male literary structures.
>
> (Barbara Smith, *But Some of Us Are Brave*, 1982, p.164)

Interest in reclaiming both individual and community leads to the adoption of the vernacular and oral storytelling modes: circling, repeating motifs, spiralling narratives. The interest in herbalism and rootworking aligns itself with the use of spirituality, magic and the metaphorical in the content and language of much work by African-American women writers. Confronting and dealing with a history of racism and sexism is a powerful motive for writing. Writers, moving through and beyond their articulated rage, celebrate difference.

BLACK WOMEN'S WRITING IN CONTEXT – READING PRACTICES

> Afro-American woman remained an all pervading absence until she was rescued by the literary activity of her Black sister in the latter part of the twentieth century.
>
> (Mari Evans, *Black Women Writers*, 1985, p.4)

This literary success, and the critical structures and frameworks which writers have helped to establish, have provided a real stimulus to writing, reading and publishing and to confirming a sense of identity for Black and Asian women worldwide. Both Black and white critics provide advice on how to be sensitive to cultural differences, as a reader and more generally. Dealing with difference springs from political, gendered, philosophical and psychoanalytical positions. As the African-American writer Audre Lorde says:

> In our work and in our living we must recognize that difference is a reason for celebration and growth rather than a reason for destruction.
>
> (Audre Lorde, *Black Women Writers at Work*, 1984, p.101)

Audre Lorde's point is powerful and liberating. It challenges Westernized imperial and colonial, polarized thought processes (Black *or* white, male *or* female, good *or* bad) which would not merely categorize as 'Other' all that is not 'self', but then produce notions of hierarchy, making the 'Other' secondary, subordinate, to be controlled, conquered, owned or destroyed. Difference should instead be a reason for celebration, argues Lorde.

Critic Cora Kaplan points out that if we are not ourselves from a particular culture, in order to read, discuss and interpret we must ourselves find out about that specific culture and the context from which the works spring:

> Unless we are actually specialist on the area from which these foreign anglophone literatures come, and teaching them in that context, our more than usually fragmented and partial knowledge of the history, politics and culture in which they were produced and originally read, frequently leads us into teaching and thinking about these texts through an unintentionally imperialist lens, conflating their progressive politics with our own agendas, interpreting their versions of humanism through the historical evolution of our own.
>
> (Cora Kaplan, *Sea Changes*, 1986, p.185)

Critical response is an important way to articulate and negotiate communication. Merely celebrating and recording, without critical response, is insulting, and 'speaking for' other people's experiences should be avoided. When we discuss and write about the writing of others hitherto marginalized, hidden and silenced we need to avoid appropriation, taking them over, feeling our critical attention is the only thing that indicates their worth.

Post-colonial critical practice should avoid seeing all women writers solely in terms of speaking from a subordinate position, and speaking out against oppression. Each writer and each context are different, and Toni Morrison's work in particular ensures that we appreciate the specificity of individuals, whose individuality and specific histories are explored, and often celebrated through this exploration. So when we want to discuss work by authors from different contexts whose lives are different from our own, how do we do that? Two critics, Gayatri Chakravorty Spivak and Sneja Gunew offer solutions:

Why not develop a certain degree of rage against the history that has written such an abject script for you that you are silenced? The problems of speaking *about* people who are 'other' cannot, however, be a reason for not doing so. The argument that it's just too difficult can easily become a new form of silencing by default... But whites can never speak *for* Blacks.

(Spivak & Gunew, 'Questions of Multiculturalism' in *Hecate*, 1986, p.137)

A whole branch of Black feminist criticism has emerged which avoids the cultural imperialism or takeover and misinterpretation possible through reading from a white or a white feminist context. This emphasizes the importance of individuality, the subject position, cultural context and difference. It celebrates the body, the sexuality, the energies of a particular Black aesthetic – recognizing that Black writers and African-American women in particular are drawing on different roots in terms of form and language, perception and experience. It recognizes the oral storytelling forms, such as testimony (the importance of the individual telling their own tale as evidence of experience), and the debating format also called 'dialogic' where different views are aired as if in a community discussion. Inheritance from the African folktale, among other forms, also makes crucially different contributions to literary development.

❋ ❋ ❋ *SUMMARY* ❋ ❋ ❋

We have looked at:

- Toni Morrison's personal life and her work – in brief;

- her influences for example, Zora Neale Hurston;

- social, political and cultural background – history of slavery, racism, Civil Rights Movement;

- Black women writers in context – reading practices;

- Black feminist criticism.

4 Major Themes

Toni Morrison is a great, late-twentieth/twenty-first century, internationally acclaimed, visionary African-American woman writer. These related definitions each provide an entry into her major concerns with themes, and with her style. Her themes focus on rewriting history, investigating and questioning stereotypes of race and gender. They provide more than a reversal of white literary and cultural versions of African-Americans, exploring links between the lived history and inner feelings and worlds of people and the narratives by which they live their lives through mixing the magical/supernatural and the historical.

THE SUPERNATURAL AND THE REAL

Morrison's work carefully rewrites hidden moments in history, discovering dates and facts, lifestyles, clothes and the paraphernalia of specific moments with great accuracy. She is equally careful to evoke the imagined lives of people at those points in history which she chooses. Morrison rightly believes that the imagined life – the life of our feelings, dreams, nightmares – is equally real to us, so by using metaphor and imagery, fantasy, the supernatural, magic and the spiritual she presents a fully rounded enriched vision of the lives and thoughts of people at different historical moments. The network of imagery within her novels and the evocation of the magical and spiritual have made some readers, who are searching for a straightforward storyline alone, find her difficult. Indeed, some early critics failed to understand that Morrison is both a recorder of Black lives and times, and a writer bent on recreating the feelings, hopes, dreams, fears, beliefs of the times and the people. To do this, she uses metaphor. While some earlier reviewers criticized her work for 'merely' recording Black lives, others failed to recognize they were reading works of the imagination, as well as historical records. In *Song of Solomon*, for example, there is the case of Pilate, a sensitive, imaginative, powerful woman. She is a herbalist, not one to bother with conformity, someone who has definitely created her own identity (as far as this is possible) against all odds and restraints. Pilate is said not to have a navel. Clearly this is physically impossible but the metaphor of not having a navel indicates that Pilate *is* her own woman – she has given birth to herself, she is an individual. Here reading as realists alone would confuse us. Morrison asks us to read as imaginative, poetic fantasists also, in order to interpret her symbols, racial and gendered stereotypes and bring individuals to life.

RECUPERATING HISTORY

Toni Morrison's work resonates with her interest in recuperating a Black American history, with recording and representing the musical and lived voices of the people, and with exploring relationships of power between white and Black, between men and women. She uses historical moments of joy and importance in Black history, many of which have been entirely hidden from the conventional history books which mainly concentrated on white, male, middle-class histories. In doing so, Morrison re-interprets the past and re-centres it – on Black experience. We read and hear about worlds and lives from which we would otherwise have been excluded and which were rarely recorded formally. She has proved a past through her imaginative reconstructions.

SLAVERY

In so doing she tackles such very sensitive issues as slavery, the slave crossing from Africa to America, and the destructive inheritance of slavery in people's minds and lives. *Beloved* imaginatively recreates a moment in history when slaves were free in the American North but still in chains in the South, and one woman, Sethe, escapes across the river, as did many others, into Ohio, to establish a new life there. In history, women such as Harriet Tubman helped slaves make this journey, their spirits upheld with song, their journeying plans and routes masked with secret codes and communications. Sethe's family, however, are sought out by a slave-catcher who wishes to 'reclaim property' and tragedy results, with a baby's death. The book, by focusing largely on the return of the baby as a fully grown woman, a ghost whose presence is felt as very real in the midst of the family, re-creates historical experiences, imagines feelings, imagination and emotions of the time. Morrison also enables us as readers and herself as a writer, to dramatize, embody and explore the reality of actually living with the legacy of slavery. In so doing, she tackles the most sensitive subject in race relations, and in the shared history of a people.

JAZZ AND THE JAZZ AGE

Morrison also looks at other periods in Black history: the Harlem Renaissance in New York, its roots, and the roots of the people in the countryside (the 1930s, in *Jazz*). When the Jazz Age arrived it gave African-Americans new opportunities for success. Musical and other talents were recognized, enabling people to hope, to gain fame and also to move into a more materialistic society. This latter issue is partly what goes wrong with the age. Morrison tackles and explores racism, both overt and covert, the latter involving ignoring people their rights, needs and histories, and silencing them through refusing to give them a voice with the vote, with publication, or with reportage in the press. So, in *Jazz*, a murder goes unreported simply because it happens in the Black community and the mainstream press finds it unimportant.

Jazz captures and re-imagines a historical and cultural moment. It restores and rewrites a hitherto largely absent Black history between the wars, the period of the Harlem Renaissance when jazz musicians gained prominence and wealth, and writing began to flower with works by both Nella Larsen and Zora Neale Hurston. The story moves from the Southern countryside where people have been sharecroppers, living in poverty, to New York, with its promises of opportunities and wealth but also its juke joints and violence, its poverty. For Black folk 'strap hanging' in trains moving on from the South to New York, the American Dream seemed to be a real promise. Toni Morrison points out that this is deceptive as the city, seeming alive, does not reward its promises.

Jazz gives us different perspectives and scrutinizes everyday African-American life. It deals with lies, rural myths vs. urban myths, suffering, power, boundaries, male–female relationships and the role of music. The three main characters, Violet, Joe Trace and Dorcas all fall victim to lies about urban success. Joe, sucked in by the possibilities offered by selling cosmetics, leaves his long-time wife, Violet, for a young woman, Dorcas, and the tale ends in tragedy. When Dorcas leaves Joe for a younger man, a sharp-suited selfish type, Joe seeks her out at a party, and in the ensuring fracas, shoots her.

While streetcars and juke joints predominate, the infrastructure which could enable economic development is missing. They have been sold a lie. The ghetto contains:

> the church, the store, the party, the women, the men, the postbox (but no high schools), the furniture store, street newspaper vendors, the bootleg houses (but no banks), the beauty parlors, the barbershops, the juke joints, the ice wagons, the open food markets, the number runner, and every club, organization, group imaginative.
>
> (*Jazz*, p.10)

POST WORLD WAR II

In *Sula*, another historical moment is explored when freed Black slaves were offered space to develop a town. Discovering that the valley space offered to these people was the most fertile, deceiving white plantation owners convinced them that they should take the barren rocky uplands calling them 'the Bottom' and claiming this meant they lay at the bottom of heaven. The town is described at different historical moments, giving us a sense of familiarity with the shops, the diners, the people who live there, so that we care when eventually the white developers decide to take over and turn it into a golf course. Initially it is described as a neighbourhood:

Just a neighbourhood where on quiet days people in valley houses could hear singing sometimes, banjo sometimes, and, if a valley man happened to have business up in those hills – collecting rent or insurance payments – he might see a dark woman in a flowered dress doing a bit of a cakewalk.

(Jazz, p. 4)

Historical details are accurate, and the people typical – women dancing in the streets with a kind of natural joy (something of a racial stereotype) – and individual – Reba's hair salon is clearly a unique enterprise. Interlaced with the descriptions, however, are implications that white people own the houses and the businesses, and that there is separation between white and Black. A predominant white version of Black is of the entertainment they might provide (dance, sex, music). Morrison always describes both factually and symbolically, her descriptions resonating with meanings and values.

INTERROGATING RACIAL AND GENDERED STEREOTYPES AND BRINGING INDIVIDUALS TO LIFE

I refuse to let them off the hook about whether I'm a Black woman writer or not, I'm under a lot of pressure to become something else. That is why there is so much discussion of how my work is influenced by other 'real' writers for example white Southern writers whom I'm constantly compared to.

(Morrison, interview with Stuart, in McKay, Nellie,
Critical essays on Toni Morrison Boston, GK Hall, 1988, p.15)

Toni Morrison declares herself to be a Black woman writer, concerned with focusing on hitherto hidden or misrepresented lives of African-American people. But her work is not separatist as such. It seeks both a Black audience and a white one, and when exposing the history and legacy of racism it does not blindly condemn all white people. Morrison understands the ways in which imaginations work and so shows her readers that those in power, of European descent, constructed for themselves a polarized response, seeing Black as opposite and less than white. Whites, Otherizing people who were different, fearing the other, sometimes demonized, controlled and tried to destroy this feared Other. This is not to excuse but to psychologically explain thought processes behind often unforgiveable behaviours and actions. The racism she exposes ranges from the inhumanities of slavery and the activities of the **Ku Klux Klan**, to behaviour which completely ignores Black people.

In *Beloved*, slavery on Sweet Home plantation/homestead destroys the men, and dehumanizes everyone. Morrison's tale emphasizes the lived presence of the legacy of slavery among all those whose ancestors have suffered it, and the poison of guilt among those who perpetrated it.

Racism causes white shop-owners to refuse to see Pecola in *The Bluest Eye*, and Pecola internalizes a negative image because of her own Blackness in the face of a society which only values blonde-haired, blue-eyed little girls, doll-like Shirley Temple types, seeing Pecola as ugly and worthless. Morrison does not just dwell on the negatives, however, she celebrates the positives. Aware of lives and strong women, she enables readers to envisage potential for change and the importance of individuals.

KEYWORD

Ku Klux Klan: established following the emancipation of the slaves in the USA, the Ku Klux Klan were, and still are, groups of whites, mostly men, whose racism and insistence of white supremacy has led to cloaking brutality with pseudo-religious behaviours and garments. Donning white sheets and hoods with cut out eyeholes and bearing burning crosses they terrorized Black men and women largely (but not uniquely) in the American South, lynching, torturing and terrifying.

CIVIL RIGHTS

In both *Song of Solomon* and *Paradise*, Morrison focuses on the 1960s, the moment of the Civil Rights Movement. Milkman Dead's friend, Guitar, is equally imaginative and violent, caught up with a group of activist, gun-carrying youth. In this period, many Black men were unable to manage their relationships with women. In the women's demands for equality they encountered challenges to their activism. They believed it necessary to prioritize politics, before coping with sexual equality, expecting women to tolerate abuse and subordinate positions because of a shared cause. A deep-rooted fear grew of women's developing feminist awareness, which emphasized the importance of motherhood, goddess religions and power. There was also, Morrison suggests, a kind of complacency about the history of African-American people, leading to an inability to see the need for change. Established ways were turning into prejudices and fixed ideas. *Paradise* is a complex book; the racism and sexism it explores are handled with imagination and insight, getting to the philosophical and psychological heart of how people think and behave.

GENDER AND STRONG WOMEN

Toni Morrison's work concentrates on gendered relations, women's lives, motherhood, sisterhood, the community, and sexual politics. Her work explores gendered relationships of individuals and communities, women and men together, and the damage people do to each other as well as the potential for change. She looks at fantasies, myths and lies which construct and sometimes constrict people, particularly those of romantic fiction and of racial and gendered subordination.

In exploring issues of gender, Morrison does not merely reverse or critique stereotypes, but recognizes and portrays new insights into the lives and strengths of Black women and Black men. Elleke Boehmer points out (in Susheila Nasta ed., *Motherlands*, 1991, p.10) that in exploring myths related to strength, patriarchal and nationalist myths have predominated in African literature, and matriarchal myths are tied up with these counterparts – strong women nurturing the next generation. Rather than merely repeating the big strong 'Mammy' myth, Morrison develops strong women who survive by 'self inventing' (McKay, 1988, p.199). They develop ways to seize their own destinies. So Paul D. in *Beloved* says 'You your own best thing' to Sethe when she has come to terms with her abused past and guilt, beginning to make her life anew through imagining it as moving forward. Sula (*Sula*), associated with water and birth imagery, grows up and becomes involved in relationships with many of the town's men, creating her own identity as an outsider, someone who cannot be pinned down. Refusing labelling, Morrison's women avoid stereotyping, claiming their own position as individuals beyond the limitations of stereotyping, offering new possibilities for revisioning – seeing anew. This also relates to the establishing of the importance of an individual, the subject, crucial in Black writing, for those who have been silenced, absent and denied an individualized voice. Baby Suggs in *Beloved* is a community leader whose capacity for storytelling and prayer unify those around her. Morrison writes about the lives of strong women, of mothers and daughters, some of whom are supportive (*Beloved*), and others who are not so (*The Bluest Eye*). She also writes about friends (*Sula*), and women whose sexuality is considered dangerous, outrageous, and/or a projection of versions of identity and self-worth.

ROMANTIC FICTIONS

In *Song of Solomon*, Hagar, Milkman's cousin, devotes herself to being his partner. His eventual rejection destroys her. At the heart of this destruction is the internalization of the belief that only with a man like 'prince charming' can she be herself and develop. Hagar's investment in the cultural myths of romantic fiction destroys her. She falls for cosmeticized lies, believing if she has a total make-over, her man might return. How could he, she thinks, looking at herself in the mirror, find her attractive, without her making all those expensive efforts that adverts tell her to make: 'Look at how I look, I look awful. No wonder he didn't want me, I look terrible' (p.309). Buying into this lie, she loses her sense of self-worth and her hold on life. The scene of Hagar impulse shopping in a systematic and overwhelming way is culturally resonant for all women who have bought these lies, and who have believed they could construct versions of identity with which they felt comfortable when in fact they were buying pre-packaged images. It kills Hagar. She dissolves as the complex, artificial make-up dissolves in the rain and the parcels leak onto the floor:

Hagar hoped shopping would change her life.

She bought a Playtex garter belt, 1. Miller No Color hose, Fruit of the Loom panties and two nylon slips – one white, one pink – one pair of Joyce Fancy Free and one of Con Brio ('Thank heaven for little Joyce heels'). She carried an armful of skirts and Evan-Picone two-piece number into the fitting room.

(*Song of Solomon*, p.311)

She is too big for most of the clothes she tries on. When she reaches the cosmetics department she is overcome by the promise, the exotic names suggesting erotic power, and money: 'Fracas, and Calypso and Visa and Bandit' (p.312).

She wants a 'beauty that would dazzle him' (p.313). Buying into an artificial culture which denies the self is destructive, the language warns, especially for women, whose vulnerability is more psychologically charged than that of the men (Milkman fights his opponents, while Hagar internalizes them and believes they are part of her self-identity, to her cost). Discovering a damaged rouged doll of a self in the eyes of her mother and sister, Hagar self-destructs. Milkman's imagined gaze has helped her construct this image – the absurdity and inappropriateness of which indicts both Milkman and material society. Hagar, like Pecola in *The Bluest Eye*, is the victim of internalizing and believing in vacuous representations, based on racial and gendered power structures.

SEXUALITY AND POWER: 'THE ERUPTIONS OF FUNK' (WILLIS, 1984)

Morrison's writing, in common with several other Black women writers such as Ntozake Shange, celebrates the erotic and the sexual 'funkiness' or liberated energies of women. Sethe recuperates a version of her own sexual self at the end of *Beloved*, and Sula looses her sexual energies on all around her, to mixed results. The women in *Paradise*, supporting other women through problems and explorations related to sexuality and sexual freedoms, place themselves outside the town's values and rules. Their alternative values directly contravene patriarchal and paternalistic controls of the men, who ignore, restrain and forbid their women any kind of control over their own bodies. Morrison's explorations of women's sexuality reveal an area related to creative energies, the claiming of identity, the recognition of self-worth.

THE SUPERNATURAL, IMAGINARY AND MYTH

Part of Morrison's aims are to critique the myth of Black inferiority and subordination which prevails in largely white culture, internalized, damagingly, by some Black people (such as Pecola in *The Bluest Eye*). Her main aim, however, is to put people in touch with myths which enable them to imagine their lives, act out their potential, recuperate and portray their inner spiritual imaginative lives, hidden often beneath historical facts, but crucial in understanding how we perceive the world, how we experience it and how we can imagine it. She says she intends to develop:

> the tone in which I could blend acceptance of the supernatural and a profound rootedness in the real time at the same time with neither taking precedence over the other. It is indicative of the cosmology, the way in which Black people looked at the world, we are a very practical people, very down to earth, even shrewd people. But within that practicality we also accepted what I suppose could be called superstition and magic, which is another way of knowing things. But to blend these two works together at the same time was enhancing not limiting.
>
> (Morrison in Evans, *Black Women Writers*, 1985, p.342)

In Morrison's work this exploration of the imaginative life, the myths and the supernatural takes several forms. One is the recuperation of imaginative histories. In *Song of Solomon*, Milkman Dead literally walks back into the landscape of his family's history seeking what he believes to be gold, but what turns out to be a more important legacy: the roots (cultural and historical) of his family. The myth of the 'flying African' runs throughout the novel, a tale of African men fleeing constraints both in terms of their enslavement and of the ties that families and communities put upon them.

Beloved recuperates the horrific past of slavery and its damaging legacy through the form of a ghost story featuring the returned, lived presence of a dead baby, Beloved (short for the religious service which begins 'dearly Beloved we are gathered here today…'), murdered by her mother, Sethe, to rescue her from a return to slavery. Morrison employs a specifically African-American version of the Latin American originated form of magic realism in writing *Beloved*. She places historical facts – the escape of Sethe's historical model Margaret Garner and her attempted killing of herself and all her children to avoid returning to slavery – alongside the metaphorical and supernatural – a baby ghost as a poltergeist and the lived presence of the baby grown-up, an adult young woman, Beloved.

MUSIC

Toni Morrison concentrates in her novels on the song, the music, the sounds of African-American women's lives. Many of her works have a focus on music, the blues, and jazz in particular as this represents the spiritual and imaginative ways in which people conceptualized and shaped their own versions of lives and their communities. Most of her novels have a shape rather like jazz music with main themes, sub-themes and a coda, and with interweaving harmonies which represent the different characters. Through the blues (*Beloved* and *The Bluest Eye*), she evokes the sufferings and stoicism of the slave years, and in *Jazz*, the moments of radical changes of the Jazz Age; representations of Black people speaking out and making a political statement as well as as a personal one.

> **KEYWORD**
>
> Magic realism: originating in the works of Latin American writers such as Gabriel Garcia Marquez from the 1960s onwards, magic realism is a form of writing combining both the factual and realistic with the magical, imaginative and supernatural. Authors show people's imaginative, lived feelings *and* what they actually say and do. It enables them to show paradox and contradictions. Great twentieth-century magic realists include Angela Carter and Salman Rushdie.

Jazz music gave everyone hope and energy.

❋ ❋ ❋ *SUMMARY* ❋ ❋ ❋

Toni Morrison's work engages with:

- recuperating history – key moments in the lives of African-Americans through history;

- investigating, interrogating and challenging racism;

- mixing the magical and the historical to portray the imaginative life;

- women's lives – motherhood, sisterhood and individuals;

- sexuality and power – 'the eruptions of funk';

- music – its importance in Black lives, its resonance and its use as metaphor.

Major Works 5

> I wrote *Sula* and *The Bluest Eye* because they were books I had wanted to read. No-one had written them yet, so I wrote them. My audience is always the people in the book I am writing at the time, I don't think of an external audience.
>
> (Morrison, in *Tate*, 1984, p.122)

In her novels, Toni Morrison focuses on the lives of African-American people in different historical periods. She engages with individuals, their families and communities, exploring their experiences in periods of history, the official versions of which tended to exclude Black people (as if they were not there – when of course, they were).

In looking at the lives of individuals in different key moments – during slavery, in the Jazz Age, in the 1960s – when people sought their historical roots, Morrison also provides insights into the ways people were thinking, their 'imaginary', their feelings, imaginations, the stories they told themselves and by which they constructed their lives. This imaginative perception, the way we see the world we are in, is represented often through magic, the supernatural and the spiritual. Morrison concentrates on the ways in which different people within or without a community engage with experiences, and how they debate and represent them, interpret and replay them, to others. Using a sense of debate, the dialogic, indicates how a community responds to something, making sense of it through discussion and storytelling. It also shows there is never only one version or imposed perception of any event.

Morrison shows that there might have been single versions of history, single sets of interpretations and values, but they have been constructed and *imposed* by a certain ruling group, in this instance white people over the lives of Black people.

Morrison shows in her work that the supernatural lives side by side with the real. For the reader, believing in this involves a suspension of disbelief, and involvement. Morrison also intends to make the stories she tells appear as if produced by the community. They are important to its sense of identity and history, and are constantly rewritten or respoken, reconstructed as different people interpret them to pass them on. This use of oral storytelling formats ensures reader/audience involvement in making meaning. It relates Toni Morrison's enterprise to that of ordinary people in many communities including African cultures, Aboriginal and working-class communities, wherever the written is not necessarily prioritized over the spoken. Today,

> **KEYWORD**
>
> Post-colonial: the Post-colonial refers to responses and behaviours produced both during and after colonial periods (when countries such as the USA and Britain colonized and ruled other countries). Post-colonial responses are reactions against or critiques of the constraints and constructions, the oppressions of colonial rule. Great post-colonial critics include Edward Said and Gayatri Chakravorty Spivak.

the professions also give new prominence to oral narrative, for example, doctors taking histories, lawyers organizing defences. Oral storytelling is a way of reflecting how we make meaning. Toni Morrison intends:

> …to make the story appear oral, meandering, effortless, spoken – to have the reader feel the narrator without identifying that narrator, or hearing him or her knock about, and to have the reader work with the author in construction of the book – is what's important. What is left out is as important as what is there.
>
> (Morrison in Evans, *Black Women Writers*, 1985, p.341)

In her work we find history and magic, oral storytelling, the sense of a dialogue between ideas, and a focus on identity, reclaiming history and giving individuals a voice.

THE BLUEST EYE

The Bluest Eye (1970) was Toni Morrison's first novel and caused much response among critics because of its direct representation of the life and perceptions of a young Black girl, rarely the central subject of fictions. Her earlier works, particularly *The Bluest Eye* necessarily, it seems, often deliver a depressingly negative message in their investigation of the lived realities of racial prejudice.

The damaging internalization of negative representations of beauty and Blackness are Toni Morrison's major focus in *The Bluest Eye*, set in 1940s Ohio, which opens with the familiar schoolbook reading primer fantasy of 'Dick and Jane'.

Style and contrasts

The first two pages emphasize the primer's story of white, middle-class children in a stereotypical family. The language is simple, accessible to children just beginning to read. The expression suddenly becomes confused, run together, no longer easily readable. This suggests the way in which a young child might read the primer, running all the words together and not making sense, but it also suggests that Pecola, a young, emotionally damaged Black girl, cannot find herself in this version of a life sharply contrasting her own abused, ignored life. Parts of the primer begin each chapter, reminding readers that African-American people from working-class origins measure themselves against, or are measured against, ill-fitting stereotypes, and so could internalize a version of falling short, not really achieving. This ironic juxtaposition of formal, white, middle-class reading primer language with that of Pecola and her abused and abusive family also reminds us how language is interwoven with power. Loss of identity, confusion, a devaluation of self emerges in Pecola's tragic story. As a tale of a girl growing up, it contrasts with more conventional nineteenth-century tales – *Jane Eyre* or *Oliver Twist* – in which individuals develop and relate to the values of their society. Here, Pecola's development is one of loss and lack of self-worth. Morrison interweaves reading primers and conventional **Bildungsroman** forms to highlight the silencing and devaluing of Black people in American society, and the resulting pains and evils of this.

KEYWORD

Bildungsroman: story focusing on the development of an individual, their growth and change as they mature. Often nineteenth-century novels used this form to show individuals developing as members of their society, surviving various perils and evils, and growing up.

Morrison shows us that one of the great losses for Black people is to internalize a version of themselves that makes them always seem lacking, just because of their colour.

Morrison's naming is always significant. The last thing this family does is breed love. Pecola's father, Cholly, was humiliated by young white onlookers while making love to his girlfriend, Darlene. This experience conditioned him to identify sex and women with humiliation and to offload his sense of shame and disgust onto women, both his wife and then his daughter, Pecola. A blind victim of racial hostility and dehumanization, he acts 'with a violence born of total helplessness' (p.137). Directing his negative self-image and disgust at women onto Pecola, he rapes her, ironically believing this shows his tenderness.

Cholly is not the only one who abuses Pecola. Her mother, Pauline favours the white children in her care over her own children. While she keeps the white household where she works in total order, maintaining her own role, she ignores her own children, making them feel they have neither love nor space.

Pecola constantly feels ignored and worthless. In one incident, a white immigrant shopkeeper treats her as entirely invisible, somehow guilty for existing:

> She does not know what keeps his glance suspended. Perhaps because he is a grown up man, and she is a little girl. But she has seen interest, disgust even anger in grown male eyes. Yet this vacuum is not new to her. It has an edge; somewhere in the bottom lid is the distaste.
>
> (*The Bluest Eye*, p. 36)

Claudia had no time for Shirley Temple white dolls, but Pecola sought blue eyes.

Pecola has only a Shirley Temple doll, icon of fairytale whiteness, and the image of blue eyes, something which should provoke love, she has been told (however, no-one can describe how to encourage love prior to the making of babies). She adores the doll as a visual representation of what girls should be, to which she aspires with an ironically desperate pointlessness. Subject to the overwhelmingly negative stereotypes of Black women and the overwhelmingly positive idealized stereotypes of white women, Pecola can only see herself as a hopeless, absurd failure. Her vulnerability is the tragedy of centuries of internalizing negative perceptions constructed by oppressors, in her case both white people and men. She is neither culpable nor guilty; how could she do otherwise? Claudia, Pecola's companion and the first-person narrator of much of the four-part novel, rejects the ill-fitting stereotypes. She would like to dismember the Shirley Temple doll and requires other representations and alternatives. In their absence she learns to lie, pretends to love:

> It had begun with the Christmas and the gift of dolls, The big, the special, the loving, gift was always a nice blue-eyed Baby Doll.

> ...Adults, older girls, shops, magazines, newspapers, window – signs – all the world had agreed that a blue-eyed, yellow-haired, pink-skinned doll was what every girl child treasured.

> > (*The Bluest Eye*, p.22)

Not finding it beautiful, she investigates its working parts, dismembering it, horrifying the adults. She 'destroyed baby white dolls' (p.22). The impulse to transfer 'to little white girls', is clearly far too dangerous and ultimately self-destructive. Collusion is a good decision for self-preservation. Claudia understands how not to be destroyed by distaste and hatred; she learns how to fit in. This is a compromise rather than a positive direction, but Claudia – intelligent, active, ironic – survives as a *positive* voice in the novel.

In Pecola's life there is no hope and no sense of worth. She is the victim of her upbringing, ignorance, disorder, lack of love, and racial distaste. When Pecola (barely twelve) becomes pregnant after her father's rape, gossips blame her and everyone wishes the baby dead.

Against such negativity, Toni Morrison describes positive female survivors, such as a trio of prostitutes, and suggests that, in the face of being ignored or silenced, some, such as Claudia, develop individuality and strength. Throughout the novel, songs of the blues are heard from Pecola's mother and others, linking this community with their history in slavery and their expression through song.

SULA

'I knew I was going to write a book about good and evil and about friendship' (Morrison in *Tate*, 1984, p.122). *Sula* (1973) is about growing up, female friendship and identity, and about a community.

It concentrates on an unconventional Black woman, Sula Peace, whose life of unlimited social and sexual experiment is unusual, outrageous, even evil. Morrison here explores how Black people accept evil as a part of their lives, and do not feel that they need to destroy it, as white people do. They have a different concept of the 'Other' – that which is socially outcast – perhaps because they have often been outcast in predominantly white society. She says:

> Black people never annihilate evil. They don't run it out of their neighbourhoods, chop it up, or burn it up. They don't have witch hangings. They accept it. It's almost like a fourth dimension in their lives. They have to protect themselves from evil, of course, but they don't have the puritanical thing which says if you see a witch, then burn it.
>
> (Morrison, in Taylor-Guthrie [ed.] *Conversations with Toni Morrison*, Jackson: University of Mississippi Press, 1994)

> White people's reaction to something that is alien to them is to destroy it. That's why they have to say Black people are worthless and ugly
>
> (*Conversations with Toni Morrison*, 1994)

Sula, defined by Morrison as a 'classic type of evil force' (*Conversations with Toni Morrison*, 1994, interview with Robert Stepto) is a pariah figure, and the Black community is also like a pariah community living apart from others. Representing what unsettles and could be considered evil, Sula also represents the community and its conscience. Evil is a fact of life, part of *them*.

Sula is a violent book. Suffering and loss are widespread. A child, Chicken Little, drowns, and others burn or disappear. People in the community need to off-load their doubts and discords onto Sula, scapegoating her. Morrison explores ways in which society constructs versions of values and reality which polarize people, defining and destroying what is different. This is the kind of self-protective exclusiveness which also produces race hatred and all hatred of difference. In *Sula*, through investigating the pariah, Morrison investigates the social forces which create one person or a group (Black Americans, women, etc.) as pariahs and as 'Other'. By exposing this, perhaps we could learn how *not* to Otherize and blame.

A historical community novel

Black feminist critic Barbara Christian sees *Sula* as a community novel: 'The novel is not only about Nel Wright and Sula Peace, it is most emphatically about the culture that spawns them' (Christian, 1985). The novel focuses on women's friendships. Sula sleeps with her best friend Nel's husband, but when she dies, Nel realizes Sula's worth. A positive force, their friendship enables them to share everything and everyone.

The novel is in ten chapters, each taking place in a specific year: 1919, 1920, 1921, 1922, 1927, 1937, 1939, 1940, 1941 and 1965. It is a historical piece with a blank at its centre (1941–65). It adopts oral storytelling forms: '*Sula* is more spiral than circular' (Morrison in *Tate*, 1984, p.122). It has a rhythm, recording the end of the community before the story begins, and suggesting events before they happen chronologically, spiralling round to fill in the details and thus creating both a sense of oral history, and lived reality. The form of the novel involves readers emotionally as if participants.

A community novel, it suggests *debates* within a community. Toni Morrison says she wanted to make the neighbourhood, Medallion, Ohio, strong, without making it quite a character. Like an African folktale, myths come to life and the past seems present. The oral storyteller spins ever intricate webs of connectiveness. But in the novel death seems to predominate. Shadrack, a shell-shocked veteran of World War I establishes 'National Suicide Day', and one-legged Eva, Sula's grandmother, can be seen as the face of death. Eva devoted her life to her children, but when she sees her son deteriorate through drug abuse, dissolving back as if into a time before birth, to 'save' him she burns him and the house down, losing her daughter in the process.

Sula and strength

Fire, water, earth and wind, essential forces of nature pervade the novel and Sula herself is seen in relationship to water (accidentally Morrison chose a name which in Tui means 'water'). She has a birthmark (Morrison's symbol of strength for Black women) like a plant and, like water, she assumes various shapes and behaviours, reinventing herself. Sula, imaginative with a gift for metaphor, and Nel, her opposite and friend, each decide to establish new behaviours and identity: 'Because each had discovered years before that they were neither white nor male, and that all freedom and triumph was forbidden to them, they had set about creating something else to be' (p.23).

The community accepts Nel and her mother Helene, but is ambivalent about the more disruptive, mercurial Sula. Fitting in is not always straightforwardly valued. Helene, on a train to the South, smiles at the train guard in a coquettish, subservient manner (recalling slavery). This moment is embarrassing for her daughter Nel, and other African-Americans around her:

> Like a street pup that wags its tail at the very door jamb of the butcher shop he has been kicked away from only moments before, Helene smiled. Smiled dazzlingly and coquettishly at the salmon-coloured face of the conductor.
>
> (*Sula*, p.21)

The novel debates, the community debates. Morrison presents us with a work which truly involves us in thinking about right, wrong, good, evil, Black, white, conformity and the radical, magic and history.

SONG OF SOLOMON

Song of Solomon (1977) rewrites a period in the mid-twentieth century when materialism took over some people's lives and when the Civil Rights Movement developed in the US. Morrison concentrates on a single family, which is both unique and representative of debates within the Black community. Macon Dead is a businessman buying into (white) middle-class values. He owns a big car but only rides out, slowly and formally, on important occasions and Sundays. Milkman, the son, is a slickly dressed, valueless young man at odds with his more politicized friend, Guitar, the radical, who plays a part in the Civil Rights Movement and eventually carries a gun. Names are always important in Morrison's novels. The family is called Dead, but their sense of identity eventually revives through Milkman's search for his family fortune, and roots. Individuals, for example Aunt Pilate and sister Corinthians, are (negatively-mistakenly) named from the Bible. Pilate, ostracized because of her alternative lifestyle, is a strong Black woman, a root-worker and herbalist. Milkman, (a name which suggests childishness, dependence on the mother) however, has a self that 'lacked coherence' (p.73). Seeking a false fortune, he retraces his family's steps through history out from the urban environment back into the rural, literally coming into contact with his roots. As his white shoes and city-slicker clothes become dirtied, he meets people who remember his grandfather and his family, escapes dangers from the landscape and wild women (Circe), and undergoes various rites of passage until he emerges with values, and a history.

Milkman Dead walked into the countryside seeking his roots.

The novel confronts racism and the dangers of violence. Down South, Milkman discovers a history of embedded racial prejudice. When his grandfather, Macon Dead, was killed because his land was in a developer's way, there were no investigations of the white land-owning family: 'Arrested for what? Killing a nigger? Where did you say you was from?' (p.233), asks the Reverend who, marching in the Armistice Day parade, was run down by a horse, so great was the white rejection of the right of Black soldiers to take part in the commemorative march. Against such racial violence, Morrison poses questions about appropriate responses. When four little Black girls are killed, Guitar and the other vengeful young men, the 'Seven Days', intend to kill white people to even the odds: 'There are no innocent white people, because every one of them is a potential nigger killer' (p.157). His view is seen as an extremist response to the sufferings and absurdities of racial inequalities.

The novel's biblical motifs blend with African myths about the need for flight, escape and self-discovery, so the ending is ambivalent with Milkman achieving a kind of flight, or death. Identity, history, roots, family and relationships run throughout this spiritual and historically politicized novel.

BELOVED

Beloved (1987) focuses on the all-pervading dehumanization of slavery through time. Dramatically it looks at its legacy, made manifest in the figure of Beloved herself. The novel articulates and embodies a history and experience which has been ostensibly, literally and 'safely' recuperated but is actually still raw. The final page claims 'it was not a story to pass on' (p.275), using an established literary trick: creating a readership *ensures* it will be passed on. *Beloved* directly confronts racism in a novel which combines lyrical beauty with an assault on the reader's emotions and conscience. It traces, embodies and focuses on the legacy of slavery, using forms derived from traditional Black folk aesthetic. It deals with the lives and history of African-American women immediately following the emancipation of slaves in the North.

Both content and form are controversial for the reader or teacher/
student, because the subject matter is stressful to read about,
confrontational, painful and the form combines historical realism with
magic and the supernatural. *Beloved* provides a powerful, engaging
model for critical issues related to our reading of Black women's
writing.

Beloved confronts racism, and the most disturbing part of African-
American history, slavery. Its exposure of the pathology and the legacy
of slavery involves the reader's emotions and, formally, the novel is
both rich and demanding to read. The story is based on the factual
account of escaped slave Margaret Garner's killing of her young child,
in the face of recapture. *Beloved* engages with history, and myth,
combining social and historical realism, overt political impetus, in its
confrontation of racism, sexism and the supernatural. A dead baby
ghost, Beloved, returns as a young woman, disrupting relationships
and nearly destroying Sethe, her mother.

Schoolteacher and authority

A warning about intellectualizing and the dangers of misappropriation
emerges from our consideration of the indictment of the slave owner,
Schoolteacher. An educator in his dehumanizing cruelty to his slaves,
he dresses up denial of human rights in the cloak of academic
authority. Schoolteacher's pupils are told to study Sethe and other
slaves by constructing lists juxtaposing their animal characteristics
with their human. He presents an authoritative version of racism, one
backed by (spurious) intellectual argument resembling arguments
slave importers used when denying the rights and humanity of those
they sold. Schoolteacher's misuse of knowledge gives him and the
white man power over those designated as only fit for scientific
categorization rather than human relationships and respect. Study in
itself is not devalued. Later, Denver's own, more enlightened studying
provides her with opportunities.

Slavery of women

As readers, teachers and students we need to contextualize the arguments in *Beloved* by discovering more about the history of slavery, the torture, murder and economic forces. The testimonies of slaves provide inside knowledge of the slave experience. Other secondary sources such as bell hooks' *Ain't I a Woman: Black Women and Feminism* (1981) provide descriptions of the institution, and the abusive treatment of slave women by slave owners. Slave women, denied family lives and abused by white owners, were forced to be 'breeders' of future slaves. This dehumanizing experience underlies Sethe's own abuse when the men beat her and take her milk. The specific location in time is also important so we need to know about the historical changes on which the period of the novel focuses (1855), when the free Northern US states gave homes to freed slaves, but the slaves were unprotected from slave-catchers crossing to recapture those who had escaped. Margaret Garner, who had escaped with her family, saw the slave-catchers coming and tried to kill her four children. The baby girl died, the boys lived. She was in history, in fact, convicted of escaping (a property issue) rather than murder.

Beloved is essentially also about the vitality and intrusiveness of memory, the memory of racial oppression under slavery. Memory or 're-memory' is acknowledged as present, solid, vital:

> If a house burns down, it's gone, but the place – the picture of it – stays; and not just in my rememory, but out there in the world... it's when you bump into the re-memory of someone else.
>
> (*Beloved*, p.36)

History, all around us, is a tangible, visible existent that a community can experience, encounter, live with. In this novel, the cruelty and absurdity upon which a capitalist society dependent on slavery is founded, translates itself into the lived madness, the haunting of the past within no. 124, the house where first Baby Suggs, the grandmother, then Sethe, the mother, her sons and Denver, her daughter, live. *Beloved* is historically situated, politically focused, but also a novel which accepts the supernatural and magic. We suspend our disbelief when we are told that the dead baby Beloved haunts the house on Bluestone, no. 124, which has a red aura, indicating a presence. The baby's presence is occasionally malevolent and spiteful and it effectively isolates Baby Suggs, the socially acceptable face of the supernatural in shared society, a community-oriented root-worker, herbalist and lay preacher. Like the community around her, however, we have problems as readers when Beloved actually appears. Beloved walks into Sethe's life at a moment of a new family harmony and sexual unity for Denver, Sethe and Paul D. Paul D. is the last of the 'Sweet Home' homestead/plantation men who reappears in Sethe's life, having journeyed a long way. Beloved, confused in her memories about who gave her clothes, taught her ways, intrudes on family harmony. She upsets Sethe's sexual relationship with Paul D. by sleeping with him and forcing him to recognize her demand that he 'call me by my name' and 'touch me on the inside' (p.120).

Sethe, who is beginning to be able to cope with memories of the slave past, and to gain a sense of wholeness through her new sexual relationship with Paul D., finds this disrupted by Beloved, who is a succubus, draining the house of love and vitality, both spiritual and physical. Beloved forms a strong bond of dependency with Denver, finally turning to Sethe when her mother recognizes her as the daughter she sacrificed. She expands as Sethe shrinks and shrivels, trying to compensate for her guilt. Horrified, on hearing Sethe's story, Paul D. leaves. At the novel's close and after the exorcism of Beloved, Sethe and Paul are reunited. They, and we, the readers, recognize that much must be acknowledged, then lived with, if sanity is to be possible.

Breaking silence
Silence and breaking silence are central issues. The bit which Paul D. is forced to wear dehumanizes him, reducing him in his own eyes below the level of Mister, the liberated rooster:

Mister was allowed to be and stay what he was. But I wasn't allowed to be and stay what I was. Even if you cooked him you'd be cooking a rooster named Mister. But wasn't no way I'd ever be Paul D. again, living or dead. Schoolteacher changed me. I was something else and that something was less than a chicken sitting in the sun on a tub.

(*Beloved*, p.72)

Paul D. is silenced, his heart holding its secrets tight like a tobacco tin. There is a debate through the novel about hiding or articulating the unmentionable histories of slavery and the community play a role in this. Beloved is manifest history, the guilt and pain of slavery as it enters personal lives causing brutal, dehumanized actions in self-defence. Those denied human rights, such as Sethe, act in a terrible fashion, but the guilt is slavery's. Focusing on the relationship of the individual to the community is crucial. The events at no. 124 are a metaphor for the suffering, memory and guilt of the Black community. First the community are jealous of Sethe's escape and unity, failing to warn her of the slave-catcher's approach. Then they feel guilty. Finally they return, support the family, driving out the ghost, utilizing a pre-linguistic community humming sound, denying the dehumanizing language of the white man, recognizing and locating the ghost of slavery. They rid Sethe's house of the draining succubus of lived guilt and pain, Beloved. They drive out her/the unmanageable pain of the past.

They stopped praying and took a step back to the beginning. In the beginning there were no words. In the beginning was the sound, and they all knew what that sounded like.

(*Beloved*, p.259)

The noise unlocks Sethe's mind, reunites her with the community. 'It was not a story to pass on' (p.275), ends the novel. But it is crucial to pass on the tale in the shape of the novel, and not let its horror undermine the ability to confront, live with and move on from memories of slavery and everyday racism. This is an empowering recognition for African-Americans, for whites, and for Sethe herself.

JAZZ

Toni Morrison's second novel in her historical trilogy about love (starting with *Beloved*) is *Jazz* (1992). *Jazz* focuses on a specific historical and cultural moment, around the 1930s, significant in African-American history when Southern Black people moved to New York, believing they could gain work, achieve success and wealth. The reality fell short of this. While a few gained recognition for their abilities – jazz musicians and singers, such as Bessie Smith (1895–1937), Billie Holliday (1915–59); artists, writers, such as Zora Neale Hurston, the author of *Their Eyes Were Watching God*; some politicians, such as Booker T. Washington – many others remained in the urban ghettos of Harlem, subject to crime and poverty. Some ran numbers (protection rackets), worked in juke joints (bars with jukebox music), and suffered deprivation and violence. There was a vibrancy

Dorcas died but her boyfriend was more worried about his clothes.

and a sense of opportunity, but many constraints. The three main characters, Violet, Joe Trace and Dorcas, are victims of lies about urban success, and each buys into the cosmetic artifice of the period.

The city is alive: 'there is no air in the City but there is breath' (p.34). It encourages love, desire and dreams, which lead to Joe being hooked on Dorcas, cosmetics, ('Cleopatra' which he sells) and fancy clothes. These cosmeticized artificial images and actions, like Hagar's shopping spree in *Song of Solomon*, represent loss of authenticity and values.

Dorcas, the main victim, is sold on the cosmeticized image of the city, and on the city slicker, Acton (a town name), whose shoes are ruined by her blood. Dorcas' death is paradigmatic of the destructive powers of the lies of urban life.

Male–female relationships
The novel also scrutinizes male–female relations, their deceits and their lasting pleasures. Joe, bored and complacent, his love atrophied, leaves Violet for Dorcas, but eventually returns, their love bolstered by a threesome relationship. Dorcas' Aunt Manfred is dangerously repressed and frozen, but Dorcas' own sexual longing for Acton is seen as false, based on appearances. The novel excavates a legendary relationship between a Black, wild, sexual woman in the rural South and a white beautiful boy, Golden Gray (child of a rich white woman and a Black man, Hunter). The relationships between Vera Louis Gray, Golden Gray and Hunter, his father, raise issues of race and race history. Golden Gray, idealized, meets, cares and calls for the Wild Woman (a mythic type), their union producing Joe. Myth and historical realism combine. Through it all the structure and language of the novel runs like a jazz tune, with solos and harmonies, themes and repeated motifs.

The promise of music
Jazz music of the Harlem Renaissance period promised social improvement to those succeeding in it, providing ordinary people with rhythm and celebration in their lives. As a structuring device, here, it provides social comment and commentary. Jazz is a mixture of the

blues, Black music, South American, Cajun, French, a true social melting pot of music, an expression beyond the pain of the blues: 'Jazz promised new freedoms, sensuality and romantic love without ties and without real loss or suffering' *Beloved* was a blues working through the ache of slavery, while '*Jazz* itself gives a voice, expression, and a form to the searchings, pains and the celebratory patternings of a specific historical moment' (Wisker, 1992, p.43). The music replicates desire and anger, enlivens, lies, lures on, lets steam out, captures the contradictions of the city, the activities of buying food, spending money, anonymity, surface values, hope. It also provides alternative, community ways of passing on information and mood, the news. Morrison both critiques the lies it seemed to offer and celebrates its potential. She shows us that Black people's lives are not considered newsworthy, hence Dorcas' murder is unreported. In form, *Jazz* is critical, it undercuts formal conventions, refuses the mystery of a detective or crime novel, but contains a crime, highlights lies of romantic fictions, mixes history with the imaginary, and is fuelled by music and dreams.

PARADISE

'They shoot the white girl first' is how *Paradise* begins. 'I wanted to open with somebody's finger on the trigger, to close when it was pulled, and to have the whole novel exist in that moment of the decision to kill or not', says Toni Morrison.

(Anna Mulrine 'This side of Paradise', US News http://www.usnews.com/usnews/issue /980119/19rew.htm)

Paradise (1998) begins in Oklahoma, 1968, in an all-Black town established by a group of men after World War II, building on an earlier 1890 settlement. This community is, they hope, insulated from the world outside where whites are dangerous: 'Out there where every cluster of white men looked like a posse' (p.4). But by 1968 the outside, Civil Rights, Black power and hippydom are creeping in. The novel is partly a religious one, and springs, Morrison says, from her wish to

The youth of the town gathered to plan vengeance on the women in the Convent.

examine three sorts of love: mother love (*Beloved*), romantic love, (*Jazz*) and the love of God for people and for other human beings. *Paradise* juxtaposes magic and the religious, spiritual, showing an all-Black Eden or paradise to be as impossible as an all-women Eden. The tragedy at the novel's heart is the need for scapegoats in times of crisis. In the difficult times of late 1960s and early 1970s, women's roles were changing fast, moving from relative equality in work with men, to women being considered as possessions within a male-dominated hierarchy. Toni Morrison does not identify with feminism any more than she does any other restrictive 'ism' or 'ist', but she does investigate relationships of power in terms of gender and race, and this is the focus of *Paradise*. With *Paradise*, Toni Morrison concentrates on the representation and treatment of women, focusing on a community, 'the Convent', of women leading alternative, feminist lives, on the edge of the all-Black pioneering town, Ruby. The women's different stories are told. Some flee from loveless relationships, oppression, excessive religious control and hypocrisy, taking refuge in the alternative ways of the Convent.

Attacking the radical women

The established ways of this town make people fiercely proud of their history and heritage, but their inability to cope with the role the women's community provides for the women of the town (escape from abuse, seeking abortion, someone to talk with), and the challenge that the mere existence of a community of women seems to pose, in the time of dominant male control, proves too much. The essential ossifying conservatism of the town, leads to the young Black men's final assault on the women's community. Fear of the power of the rather alternative women leads the men to characterize them as evil witches, blaming them for all that goes wrong in this too incestuous, old-fashioned, patriarchal, paternalistic town:

> It was a secret meeting, but the rumours had been whispered for more than a year. Outrages that had been accumulating all along took shape as evidence. A mother was knocked downstairs by her cold-eyed daughter. Four damaged infants were born in one family. Daughters refused to get out of bed. Brides disappeared on their honeymoons. Two brothers shot each other on New Year's day... So when nine men decided to meet there they had to run everybody off the place with shotguns... the one thing that connected all these catastrophes was in the Convent. And in the Convent were those women.
>
> (*Paradise*, p.11)

Attacking the women, white and Black, the men feel they have God on their side:

> Bodacious Black Eves unredeemed by Mary, they are like panicked does leaping toward a sun that has finished burning off the mist and now pours its holy oil over the hides of game.
>
> God at their side, the men take aim. For Ruby
>
> (*Paradise*, p.18)

In 'Otherizing' the women of the convent, the men find a scapegoat for the internal rot which produces malformed babies, early deaths and disagreements. There is no resolution, only conflagration – the Convent once scapegoated, will be destroyed. For the reader it is clear that those who destroy its mixed race, semi-religious, alternative existence retain their own problems.

The Convent was a place for sanctuary and sisterhood.

That even initially powerful, free-thinking Black communities can lose energy and momentum, turn to oppression and hypocrisy, lose their way, is one warning message of the novel. Another indicates how conventional patriarchal beliefs figure questioning and free-thinking women as a threat to be destroyed. The novel ends where it begins, with the raid on the Convent. The novel's message lasts, but no utopian ending is provided within it.

Paradise met with a very mixed reception – Morrison herself says she would have liked to have had a little longer working on it – but it is a powerful book. It is difficult, partly because of the complexity of the writing, but also because of the difficulty readers have with facing up to the issues that Morrison deals with – particular moments of Black Civil Rights and gendered politics. Morrison says that she is not going to avoid issues '…and say, once again, it's going to be all right, nobody was to blame and I'm not casting blame. I'm just trying to look at something without blinking, to see what it was like, and how that had something to do with the way we live now. Novels are always inquiries for me.' (The *Salon* interview: http://www.salonmagazine.com/boks/int/1998/02/cov-si-02int.html)

* * *SUMMARY* * *

- *The Bluest Eye* has an experimental form, focusing on issues of racial inequality, internalized feelings of being second-rate which destroy people, and the life and identity of a working-class Black girl.

- *Sula* provides alternative histories of African-American people in a specific town, considering people's subversive energies and myths, a 'bad' woman and her community role as outsider.

- *Song of Solomon* concentrates on rediscovering history and African roots through quest, magic and relationships in the 1950s and 1960s.

- *Beloved* is a ghost story dealing with the historical past, focusing on history recuperated, living with slavery, memory and magic.

- *Jazz* looks at Harlem and the Jazz Age.

- *Paradise* focuses on religion, and on the dissipating energies of an old-fashioned Black community during the Civil Rights Movement, looking at their inability to live alongside a community of women constructed as outsiders.

Contemporary Critical Approaches

Early reviews of Morrison's work failed to focus on the quality of the form and style and misunderstood her use of African mythology or oral storytelling, and her mixing of the magical and the historical real. They also tended to typecast her as *only* a Black woman writer (i.e. *only* dealing with issues of interest to Black readers) and then to prescribe what kinds of writing that should entail.

Toni Morrison's fine blend of the magical/supernatural/spiritual with the imaginative and metaphorical and with the historical and realistic has caused some criticism among those who would seek to limit Black women's writing to testimony and record alone. This kind of restraint upon form and language is yet another covert example of racism: subordinating others' voices and expression. Embarrassing critical comments, such as Sara Blackburn's review of *Sula*, are evidence of limited, imperialist thinking:

> Toni Morrison is far too talented to remain only a marvellous recorder of the Black side of provincial life, might easily transcend that early and unintentionally limiting classification 'Black woman writer' and take her place among the most serious, important and talented American novelists.
>
> (Blackburn, *New York Times Book Review*,
> 30 December 1973, p.3)

Immediately following the awarding of the Nobel prize for *Beloved*, some reviews indicated that Black women writers such as Morrison should concentrate on representing a factually realistic world, failing to understand the metaphorical, imaginative qualities in Morrison's work.

More positive critics related her to some of her literary forbears but concentrated on white male writers from the South, particularly Faulkner (on whom Morrison did her MA dissertation).

RACE ISSUES

John Leonard notes Morrison's first beautifully crafted novel, *The Bluest Eye*, deals with institutionalizing taste and the ways US culture defines as waste those who are not blonde and blue-eyed (*New York Times*, 13 November 1970, p.70). Several critics focused on the truth of Pecola's sense of lack of self-worth as measured against white norms, one critic even suggesting it should be read by social workers with young adults. Anne Z. Michelson takes a more positive note. Looking at literature by people who are thought of as 'socially marginal', Morrison communicates the pain of the hidden, challenging traditional assumptions about their abilities and worth ('Winging Upward Black Women: Sarah E Wright, Toni Morrison, Alice Walker', in *Reaching Out: Sensitivity and Order in Recent American Fiction by Women*, Metuchen, N.J. & London: Scarecrow Press, 1979, 124–53). This more positive reading of Morrison's work focuses not just on negative stereotypes and waste but on the aspirations of young women such as Sula and Nel (*Sula*), and Pilate (*Song of Solomon*). Pilate refuses social constraints, cuts her hair, becomes a bootlegger making liquor. In harmony with nature, she helps Milkman find his family roots and values. Michelson sees Milkman's odyssey across Pennsylvania and Virginia as picaresque in form, a series of tests of character. It is pointed out that the flight of men leaves people in suffering, while Pilate's groundless flight, one of self-assertion not escape, is nurturing and more positive.

Odette C. Martin's 'Sula' (FW, winter 1977: 35–44) sees the women Eva, Hannah, Sula and Nel as 1960s 'examples of Langston Hughes' term "special Negritude"'. Other reviewers have spotted conventions, for example, 'the tragic Mulatto', 'the Black mother/son', 'the primitive and exotic', the 'Harlem Renaissance', 'the Folk trend' and so on, but the characters, particularly Sula, critique such idealized versions of Black values. They establish their *own* identity. Sula does not have to conform, she is unique, the 'potential: the raw energy of Life and the creative impulse of Art' (p.41). *Sula* is a stern call to readers to reject suicidal powerlessness and to stop saying, 'ain't nothin' I can do about it' (p.42). The novel testifies that art should make life more meaningful, implying 'constructive self-criticism is the best, perhaps the only way to ensure that we also confront white racism directly' (p.44).

Sula is seen as challenging, offering a critique of stereotypes. Black women and Black lives are recognized as the themes in *Sula* by Douglas O'Connor ('Sula' in *BIC Annual 6*, 1974–75). Chikweyne Okonjo Ogunyemi, 'Sula: "A Nigger Joke"' reads the tale as reviving comfort through laughter, seeing it as an example of how wit and humour can meet people's needs if their dreams are deferred (*BALF* 13, 1979).

WOMEN AND GENDER

Critics are divided about Toni Morrisson's treatment of women and of Black women. Some argue she reinforces stereotypes and others that she develops positive images of strong women. As a Black woman writer, Toni Morrison provides a particular focus on women's roles and the 'triple burden' of African-American women, offering critiques of stereotypes and opportunities for women to develop self-identity, and women-oriented relationships with family and friends and the community. Her work suggests opportunities to re-value women's traditional skills, e.g. root-working, midwifery and herbalism. Many reviewers consider ways in which Toni Morrison critiques stereotypes, even those of Black people established in the **Negritude** movement of the Harlem Renaissance (1920s and 1930s).

KEYWORD

Negritude: the period of the 1930s in New York when Black people began to have their creative talents recognized and rewarded is called the 'Harlem Renaissance'. One set of beliefs which developed was that of 'Negritude' which derives from the word 'negro' and defines and celebrates some specific qualitites of being Black. These qualities help define people but they can also be racial stereotypes.

They focus on how she criticizes cosmeticized and racist images of beauty, the destructive stereotypes which construct women in roles such as whore, Mammy and so on. Morrison offers alternatives, explores friendships and relationships, such as that of mother and son, mother and daughter, and sexual relationships where women make their own choices. In recognizing this, some critics relate Morrison to other Black women writers and other women writers, emphasizing her particular contribution.

Jerilyn Fisher compares Morrison's work with that of other African-American and Chicano women, finding that women counter the effects of male dominance by forging relationships with other women ('From Under the Yoke of Race and Sex: Black and Chicano Women's Fiction of the Seventies', *MV 2*, Fall, 1978: 1–12). Fisher sees Pilate, Hagar and Reba as a loose mix of supportive women (*Song of Solomon*), and says that audacious 'maverick' characters such as Pilate and Sula (*Sula*) offer incitement to readers to battle against sexual expression and be more daring in attempts at self-achievement and sexual freedom. Fisher places Morrison's work in the history of the Black Civil Rights movement where tensions exist between discovery of roots and escape from negative histories of slavery.

FORM AND STYLE

Several early reviewers found Toni Morrison's forms confusing, particularly her mixture of the realistic and the fantastic. Some miss her deliberate use of oral storytelling forms, and her questioning of stereotypes. Chikweyne Okonjo Ogunyemi recognizes *The Bluest Eye* as a highly structured novel dealing with lack of structure in Pecola's life, and with oppressed Blacks in America more generally ('Order and Disorder in Toni Morrison's *The Bluest Eye*', *Crit* 19, 1977: 112–120). He notes the themes announced in the primer which emphasize a gap between Pecola's life and that of the white, middle-class family, a lie foisted on Americans. He comments on the treatment of sex, racism and death, the three Black prostitutes, the three scapegoat rituals, and the three types of Black women. As in James Baldwin's *Go Tell it on the*

Mountain, Pecola is a nominally main character but also a 'centripetal' force bringing all the different characters together. Her madness is mechanically motivated. Ogunyemi believes Toni Morrison has inadequately transformed notions of race from Herntson's *Sex and Racism in America*. Others criticize her treatment of Black characters, seeing them as stereotypical and trapped.

William Francis finds *Sula* disappointing, seeing the minor characters as grotesque or stereotypical, the form chaotic and confusing. He misses the deliberate oral storytelling, the circularity and the relationship of Sula to her community as a pariah who is formed from the community to enable it to see itself, (William A.C. Francis' 'Sula', *Best Sellers* 33, 15 January 1974: 469).

On the other hand, in a more sensitive critique, Margo Jefferson recognizes the achievements of Morrison as her ability to write across formal constraints – writing with accuracy both politically and historically as well as writing philosophically and passionately ('Toni Morrison: Passionate and Precise.' *Ms* 3, December 1974: 34–38). Jefferson notes that Morrison's work challenges the big assumptions that marginalized people, including Jews, women and Black people, cannot take a great part in literary texts, pointing out that the language of both *The Bluest Eye* and *Sula* is 'passionate and precise; lyrical and philosophical' (Jefferson, p.34). Morrison, she argues, is interweaving tones, textures, versions of sexual relations, balances and characters like a musician. The language is considered wonderful, particularly small phrases such as 'nuns go by as quiet as lust'.

* * *SUMMARY* * *

● Some rather crass initial responses saw her as needing to 'move on' beyond merely dealing with African-American lives and histories. Morrison wants to be recognized as a Black woman writer *and* a writer of excellence in a changing mainstream.

● What gradually develops is a celebration of Morrison's talent and her different style – combining magic and history, her engagement with recuperating hidden histories and speaking out against racism and sexism.

● Critics recognize and debate her treatment of individuality, of women's self-esteem, and of issues of race.

Modern Criticism

7

The appearance of the award-winning *Beloved* in 1987 firmly established Toni Morrison's already great reputation and ensured that critics focused less on considering her as anomalous as a great Black writer and more on her individual merit as a novelist and essayist, and as a model leading the way for recognition of other African-American women writers. Some of the issues critics have focused on since the 1980s, and most particularly since *Beloved*, are:

* issues of identity, self, and biography

* Black women's writing issues and Black women's criticism

* Morrison as a writer of magic realism who mixes history, the spiritual and the supernatural

* Morrison's postmodernism and her dialogic writing.

ISSUES OF IDENTITY, SELF AND BIOGRAPHY

'Writing the self', or writing about the self in order to establish a sense of self-worth, and claiming identity are crucial elements in the work of Toni Morrison as they are in that of many African-American and other Black writers. Testifying, testimonies of personal history and the claiming of the importance of the individual self, are important missions, affecting forms of writing. Much of Morrison's work is in storytelling form, employing the first-person narrative to guarantee a sense of authenticity. These forms, springing directly from the slave narratives of history, challenge postmodernist critical beliefs and practices. They also act out or embody some arguments found in Black women critics such as Barbara Smith and Barbara Christian, who point out that towards the end of the twentieth century Western thought processes and Western literary criticism worked together to deny the existence of the individual subject, the unique identity of individual people. Some critics and philosophers argue that we are all constructed from the influences and models around us – that we perform roles and identities. Such a set of beliefs about performance and lack of a subject position is directly in opposition to the need for Black people to assert their individual identities after years of absence and silence.

BLACK FEMINIST AND FEMINIST CRITICAL APPROACHES

Many **feminist critics** have written about the work of Toni Morrison, concentrating on her focus on Black women's lives, rescuing women from silence and absence in history. Morrison both exposes the sufferings undergone by women and celebrates strong women.

Some feminist critics argue for radical separatism, believing that men and women are totally different and women's strength emanates from their refusal to work, live with, or draw from the productions and forms of man in life and art. Others, however, recognize that men and women have different perspectives but draw language and experiences essentially from the same cultures. Men and women, they argue, have had much the same education, read the same kinds of books, so their language and forms will *not* necessarily be vastly different.

Feminist critics focus on Morrison's treatment of women and of gendered relations. For example, Wisker (1993, 2000) considers the treatment of Sethe's self-worth (*Beloved*) and Morrison's treatment of identity, gendered relations, and mothering, taking a feminist approach, placing Morrison in context of other Black and Asian women writers (for example, Emecheta, Desai).

> **KEYWORD**
>
> Feminist critics: focus on the roles of women, the representation of women (or lack of that representation) in history, culture, the arts, and issues and practices to do with women's lives. Feminist criticism considers such issues as romantic fictions, motherhood, performance, constraints by patriarchy and paternalism, and restrictions upon women's individuality and sexuality. It argues for a women-oriented language, suggesting that women, because they have had different experiences to men – i.e. have been more subordinated, less wealthy, more involved in caring for others, denied speech – are likely to favour different subject matter and to choose different language items and forms to those chosen by men.

Black feminist critics

Black feminist critics argue it is inappropriate to say that white, liberal, middle-class feminism can define the range of experiences, the validity of those experiences, and the range of expressions available to all women. Such approaches to feminism miss out the cultural and economic differences Black women face. The *Feminist Review* issue 'Black Feminist Perspectives. Many Voices, One Chant' (volume 17, 1984) explores definitions of Black feminist experiences distinct from white feminist experiences.

Many African women, for instance, are both aware of the constraints of idealizing mothering, relegating women to one specific role, but recognize value in childbearing powers and their children surrounding them as they work. Other Black women have insisted that white feminist criticism ignores the erotic, the sensuality, of some Black women's versions of feminism, and also ignores differences in economic position suffered by Black women. White feminists make statements and choices which themselves depend upon a certain standard of living not enjoyed by Black women, feminists or otherwise. In the early 1980s, Black feminist criticism started to become clearly established. It recognized different cultural and subject positions occupied by white and Black women, and expressed by Black women writers. Black feminist critics also recognized specifically women-oriented and African-originated forms of expression and narrative such as oral storytelling, circular forms and personal testimony.

The development of a Black feminist criticism by (among others) Barbara Smith and Barbara Christian, led to further recognition of Toni Morrison's work. Barbara Christian sees Toni Morrison's central theme in *The Bluest Eye* to be a search for beauty in a world which lacks beauty. Pecola lacks a sense of her own value. Like society around her that has copied white values and versions of beauty, she fails to develop a sense of her own individual worth or to recognize beauty in her Blackness.

Black feminist critical approaches usually focus on Toni Morrison's portrayal of strong women characters and on her interest in self-definition and self-development among young girls such as Pecola and Claudia (*The Bluest Eye*), Sula (*Sula*), and Hagar (*Song of Solomon*). They comment on mothering and motherhood, such as Sethe's protection of her children as a fierce, loving mother which results in her attempts to kill them rather than letting them be taken back to slavery (*Beloved*).

In *We Was Girls Together* (1982), Anna Shannon sees Morrison's fiction as 'separatist' involving characters' journeys towards identity. As early as 1974, Barbara Smith's emphasis on Black feminist critical approaches to Morrison identified links between Black women and a concentration on Black experience in the novels ('Beautiful, Needed, Mysterious', *Freedomways, 14*, 1974: 69–92). In 1979 in *Towards a Feminist Criticism*, Smith defined a 'second wave' of Black feminism, the first having begun with Francis Harper in the nineteenth century. Smith's function as a critic is political and propagandist, attacking the assumption of the Black community that sexist oppression against women either does not occur or does not matter, and pointing out that in earlier movements, such as the Harlem Renaissance and the Civil Rights Movement of the 1950s and 1960s, Black women's rights were ignored. Assertions that Black women's writing and lesbian writing need recognizing underlie her work. Smith argues that literary theory which can deal with Black feminist literature must recognize that Black women writers 'constitute an identifiable literary tradition' (p.37). Gender is as important a critical issue as race and class, and passionate friendships, including lesbian relationships, must be recognized within texts.

Critics see *Sula* as a crucial novel in the development of Black women's writing. Morrison's and Smith's work, alongside Alice Walker's, brought African-American and Black women's writing into the lives of millions. They also emphasize and celebrate how such writing and vision differs from works in the (largely white, male, middle-class) literary canon.

Jennifer Uglow ('The Folk at the Bottom', *TLS*, 19 December 1980, p.1442), sees Toni Morrison's work as highly individualistic, lacking in love and affection, filled with 'laughter that recognizes a grim bad joke'. She argues that *Sula* and *The Bluest Eye* look with ambivalence at the force of traditions familial and racial, noting the past must be passed on without the humiliation that has been inherent in it, so Morrison's work both 'explain/s/ the power of and give/s/ the lie to the cult of 'Black is beautiful'.

TONI MORRISON AS A SPECIFICALLY BLACK WRITER

Tar Baby was seen by many critics as focusing on the issue of race. Carol Rumens, ('Conflicts of Complexion', *TLS*, 30 October 1981, p.1260), says that Toni Morrison polarizes issues of racial conflict focusing the reader's attention on unresolved conflicts within and between different personalities, particularly Margaret Street, the outcast in wealthy white society, and Jadine Childs who has 'passed' in white culture. Jadine is an educated, pale-skinned Black who has a passionate affair with Son, a fugitive who taunts her with being the mythic tar baby, which itself was, in folklore, a trap created by white farmers. Rumens, a poet herself, identifies this as a highly **symbolic** novel which uses **metaphor**.

Rumens contributes to the developing focus on Morrison's writing craft. Norris Clark ('Flying Back: Toni Morrison's *The Bluest Eye*, *Sula* and *Song of Solomon*', in *MV* 4, Fall, 1980, p.51–63) defines Toni Morrison as a Black writer in terms of subject matter, forms and style, developing Black feminist arguments of Barbara Christian and Barbara Smith. Melvyn Bragg, ('Black Bottom' *U.S.A. Punch*, 5 November 1980), argues Morrison provides excursions into 'new countries'. She is like 'Faulkner turned inside out', showing that, like Steinbeck and Faulkner, Black people, 'digested the American experience and turned it into art'.

> ## KEYWORDS
>
> Symbol and metaphor: these are figures of speech. A symbol suggests or stands for something else, defines or helps the reader picture it. For example, the cross symbolizes, suggests or stands for Christianity, and water suggests or stands for life, change, movement and flow.
>
> A metaphor is an imaginative comparison of one thing with another enriching both parts of the comparison. For example, the imagination could be compared to a flying bird or a growing plant, because it develops, changes and creates. Symbols tend to be widely understood and produced by cultures while metaphors are localized in specific examples.

TONI MORRISON AS A WOMAN WRITER

Faith Pullin argues 'the task of the contemporary Black female writer is to resist imposed definitions' ('Landscapes of Reality: The Fiction of Contemporary Afro-American Women', in A. Robert Lee *Black Fiction: New Studies in the Afro-American Name Since 1945*, 1980, p.180) offering new, more accurate definitions and information. Morrison is placed in a history running from the Harlem Renaissance writers Zora Neale Hurston and Nella Larsen, to her contemporary, Alice Walker. Her denial of stereotypical destructive versions of Black women is emphasized in accounts of sexuality, breakdowns and challenges to self-esteem posed by negative versions of women's skin colour and of their beauty. Sula Peace in *Sula* is so experimental that she forces readers to reassess concepts of love and relationships between the individual and the community. Morrison, like Alice Walker, Maya Angelou and Gayl Jones, develops new approaches to social, sexual and psychological reality.

MYTHS, SYMBOLS AND IMAGERY

Much criticism of Morrison's work considers her use of myths, symbols, imagery, the supernatural and magic. Some reviewers find it difficult to deal with this mixture of mythical with history; others provide a systematic tracking through the symbolic structures relating these to Morrison's arguments about self-worth, flight, Black and white, discovering roots, questioning polarized values, and so on. Some are merely rather mechanistic analyses, while others link Morrison's work with the African myths from which her work derives in part and also recognize the musical, close relationships between content, intention and use of spirituals, blues and jazz to her themes and arguments.

Hovet and Lounsberry ('Flying as a Symbol and Legend in Toni Morrison's *The Bluest Eye, Sula* and *Song of Solomon*', 1983, p.119–40) consider Toni Morrison's use of flight symbolism to suggest freedom or moral and spiritual ascendancy, mentioning the song 'swing low sweet chariot' as an escape from the physical world to God. Flight, they argue, also appears in *The Bluest Eye*: Pauline is seen as a fallen bird, 'never fully metamorphosing to flight', and sexuality is associated, in a religious sense, with a fall (p.124). They see Nel in *Sula* as a flightless nester and Sula in sexual 'free fall' leading to isolation and death. However, comments linking sexual and individual self-awareness to flight are contrasted with Milkman Dead in *Song of Solomon* who possibly achieves flight.

In looking at *Song of Solomon*, Bonnie Barthold considers how Africans experience time as cyclic ('Toni Morrison, *Song of Solomon*', 1980, *Black Time, Fiction of Africa, the Caribbean and the US*, Yale University Press). In a literary form uncommon among Westerners, the cyclic form explains historical resistance to slavery and blends African and religious imagery and references. The form focuses on time as a location for conflict between the Western and the African. Milkman Dead in *Song of Solomon* is caught between a fragmented version of time from his father and a unified one from his Aunt, Pilate. Music is crucial and the novel works towards resolution, fusing the past and the African-American present into a song of heritage, building throughout the novel on the initial establishment of relationship between the biblical 'Song of Solomon' and the song of Sugarman, the 'flying African'.

Flight, music and myth re-emerge in the discussion of Morrison's later works. Marion Treby (unpublished PhD thesis, Cambridge, 2001) develops a thorough and systematic tracing of the musical references that underlie Morrison's argument, her record of African-American history and the individual, and her forms. Toni Morrison, she argues, breaks new ground in the use of the picaresque in women's writing. Uniquely, she traces jazz riffs and movements in *Jazz*, the blues in *Beloved* and *The Bluest Eye*, and the use of popular soul music of the 1960s in *Paradise*.

E.S. Duvall (*Song of Solomon*, ATL 240, October 1977, p.105) sees Morrison using the 'roots' myth (a search for heritage and ancestry which has been popular since the 1960s among African Americans) and quests locating Milkman Dead as finding familial roots in his quest. Susan Blake ('Folklore and Community in *Song of Solomon*, 1980) identifies sources for *Song of Solomon* in a Gullah folktale concerning African slaves who fly back to Africa, focusing on communal activities and ancestral links. Jacqueline De Weever identifies a whole host of Western myths within the novel ('Toni Morrison's Use of Fairy Tale, Folk Tale and Myth in *Song of Solomon*, 1980), including 'Rumpelstiltskin', 'Hansel and Gretel', and 'Jack and the Beanstalk'.

COLOUR IMAGERY

Bonnie Shipman Lange in 'Toni Morrison's Rainbow Code' (*Crit* 24, Spring 1983, pp.173–81), looks at the systematic use of colour imagery in Morrison, mentioning Pecola's desire for blue eyes (*The Bluest Eye*), Eva dreaming of a red dress the night before Hannah dies in the fire (*Sula*), and Macon Dead's fear of a voodoo doll with its belly painted red (*Song of Solomon*). Colour imagery is linked to Toni Morrison's development as an author, and Lange suggests that, later, Morrison uses yellow, silver and gold.

Karen Stein ('I Didn't Even Know His Name, Naming in Toni Morrison's *Sula*', in *Names*, 1980), focuses on the importance of naming as a source of power and control, concentrating on Ajax and Sula Peace in *Sula*. Equally Ruth Rosenberg looks at names in *Song of Solomon*, noting those with religious significance such as 'Corinthians' and 'Pilate', those with post Civil War Southern names, and those imposed by white officialdom thus suggesting arguments about historical and mythical roots in the narrative ('And The Children May Now Know Their Names, Toni Morrison's *Song of Solomon*', *LOS* 8, 1981, pp.195–219).

FORM

As Morrison's reputation became established, more work focused on her form and its roots, developing recognition of her deliberate use and evolution of oral storytelling forms, and opposing the early critiques of her 'chaotic forms'. One insightful comment (Susan Lardner, 'Books, Word of Mouth', *NYorker* 53, 1977), recognizes use of similes and catalogues, and how the novel is pitched at the ear. Dorothy Lee considers symbolic journeys, use of mythical names such as Circe, and dual levels of prose – the symbolic and immediate reality ('*Song of Solomon*: To Ride The Air', *BALF* 16, 1982, pp.64–70).

TONI MORRISON AS POSTMODERNIST MAGIC REALIST

Critics who began to appreciate Morrison's rich mixture of the supernatural and the real historical did so with *Song of Solomon*, but most particularly with *Beloved*. They saw Morrison's achievement in her aim to portray the imaginative life as equally important to that of the everyday, factual, action-oriented life lived with others.

Margaret Atwood ('Haunted by their Nightmares: *Beloved*', NYTBR, 13 September 1987, pp. 1, 49–50) recognizes *Beloved* as a ghost story depicting a fractured family suffering under slavery and finds the book hard on white characters but balanced overall. She notes folklore concerning the dead which operates in the novel, seeing the novel ending on a message of acceptance. Ann Snitow ('Death Duties, Toni Morrison Looks Back in Sorrow', *VV*, Literary Supplement 8, September 1987) sees *Beloved* as part of the holocaust genre of great loss and a need to exorcize in order to move on. Among other critics contemporary with the reception of this great novel, Snitow is at ease with and can provide a sensitive critique of Morrison's use of the supernatural to deal with the unpalatable and unspeakable in *Beloved*. The ghost of Beloved brings the slave experience to life, it 'makes thematic sense' (p.26) and can be seen as a rich poetic piece. Snitow disagrees with Stanley Crouch (in *The New Review*, 1987), who asserts that Morrison stereotypes and simplifies complex human emotions and, brutally, that Morrison merely writes a 'Blackface holocaust novel'. Many critics found the novel startling and stunningly written.

Two essays on *Beloved* appear in *Insights into Black Women's Writing* (Macmillan, 1993), one by Elaine Jordan and one by Gina Wisker.

Wisker's 'Dismembered and unaccounted for' focuses on the difficulties of reading a magic realism and historical mixture, and the importance of re-memory, on overcoming the 'disremembering' of hidden slave histories, recuperating, understanding the past, mourning, and moving on, for both Black and white. Morrison, as a Black woman writer, deals with Black women's history, using oral storytelling, folklore, the community, mothering and a mix of magic and history.

GENERAL TEXTS

Following the publication of *Beloved*, Toni Morrison's work has been a central focus of several books dealing with African-American women's writing and magic realism. She has had several books devoted to her work alone. Jill Matus' *Toni Morrison* (Manchester University Press, 1998), takes a specifically culturally contextualized approach, focusing on issues of racial and national identity, gender and sexuality. Matus sees Morrison dealing with this trauma, building on W.E. Dubois pointing out that American history excluded African-Americans who then appeared as a 'swarthy spectre' like Banquo in *Macbeth*, always there and yet excluded. Morrison's focus in her lectures and her essay, *Playing in the Dark* (1989), is to argue that what is defined as history is not *all* there is to know and depends on excluding Black and African history. Matus' book traces African-American history and culture as dealt with in Morrison's work. She sees that characters in *Jazz* are haunted by traumatic past experiences and also seem to have to relive them. She acknowledges the importance of jazz as a motif and a means of relating the history of excluded but energetic peoples: 'Morrison's history of the jazz age is an attempt to exorcise and assimilate the pain of the past but also to acknowledge the agency and power of its inheritors to make and relive it' (Matus, p.144).

Wisker deals with Morrison in terms of African-American history, women's writing developments, magic and the supernatural, in *Postcolonial and African-American women's writing: a critical introduction* (Macmillan, 2000) considering the full range of her work, mothering and motherhood, Black women's writing and Black feminist criticism in relation to Morrison. Wisker places Morrison in the context of other African-American, Black and Asian women writers. Linden Peach's *Toni Morrison* (1995) begins by contextualizing Morrison in history, that of US writers, and magic realism. Taking each novel in chronological order, he weaves through the variety of critical views available on Morrison's work, establishing arguments about the importance of the verbal, of rescuing silenced narratives, the complexities of historiography or historical recording of particular periods in history which largely ignore Black experience and which Morrison recuperates. Peach's edited *Toni Morrison: Contemporary Critical Essays* is wide-ranging, establishing her work as worthy of a variety of readings.

PARADISE

Paradise (1998) met with a mixed reception, partly because of its mixture of the biblical with the revolutionary, and the way it put gender and ethnicity into a spotlight, often in opposition, it seems. Louis Menand (*New Yorker*: Amazon Review, September 1999), sees it as 'the strangest and most original book that Morrison has written', noting 'Paradises are not so easily gained' and seeing the novel as powerful.

Anna Mulrine finds the book exciting, the prose difficult, and readers divided. But, she argues, in her 66 years, the sharecropper's granddaughter from Lorain, Ohio, has acquired the stature to absorb most criticism. 'I've stopped dreaming about kneecapping,' Morrison jokes. In fact, she would rather have people grapple with her work than merely revere it. 'I have people tell me, "Your novel is on my bed stand". I don't want books to be what people dip into before they go to sleep'. (Morrison interviewed by Mulrine in http://www.salonmagazine.com/boks/int/1998/02/cov-si-02int.html)

Morrison says that her characters suffer but also learn. 'It's true (my characters) go through difficult circumstances' but finally 'people always know something profound and wonderful' (*USA Today*, Deirdre Donohue, 20 September 1999. 'Morrison's slice of "Paradise"' http://www.ustday.com/life/enter/boks/b128.htm). What is powerful as well as confusing is the way in which Morrison sees the pioneering town, Ruby, as having become a little complacent. It is challenged and tested but as yet unable to channel the radical power of Black youth in the 1960s and 1970s. The town is set against the women who have established an alternative spiritual, magical, nurturing, diverse community, warts and all, on its border. Their positioning makes them more vulnerable as well as able to represent and absorb deviant energies arising from such a constrained and repressive town. Rebellion brings them out of town to the women's Convent, but this is a threat. Toni Morrison sets Black against female in a rather raw confrontation. It is a novel of confrontations and contradictions posing problems about the usefulness of fantasies and mythical histories.

Richard Eber (*The Los Angeles Times Sunday Book Review*, 1999) said of *Paradise*: 'It's a fascinating story, wonderfully detailed by Morrison's shrewd and vivid portraits of Ruby's citizens and forebears. But the author has done more than that. Her town is the stage for a profound and provocative debate – always personified and always searching – about Black identity and destiny in America's past and present'.

* * *SUMMARY* * *

This chapter has looked at:

• a firm establishment of Morrison as a key writer in the developing work of African-American writers;

• biographical readings and those establishing the primacy of the subject or the individual;

• feminist critical and Black feminist critical approaches;

• issues of stabilizing identity and self-worth, the specific roles of Black women;

• post-colonial readings noting issues of race and history, identity, and addressing cultural stereotypes;

• structural and formal readings, which emphasize imagery, structures, musical references and forms;

• critical appraisal of certain themes and contributions, for example the musical nature of Morrison's works;

• postmodernist readings which recognize the dialogic and deconstructive nature of her work, its new structural combinations and use of African forms.

What Next? 8

One piece of advice is to read more by Toni Morrison and also by other African-American women writers. Go and see the filmed version of Toni Morrison's novel *Beloved*, directed by Jonathan Demme and produced by Oprah Winfrey (1999), and her play *Dreaming Emmett* (1985), and read her critical work such as *Playing in the Dark: Whiteness and the Literary Imagination* (1985). These set a context and establish some focus for the critical appreciation of writing by African-Americans and other Black and Asian writers.

OTHER AFRICAN-AMERICAN WOMEN WRITERS

Zora Neale Hurston (1891–1960) was fortunate in being brought up in an all-Black township, Eatonville, where seeing Black people in varied jobs as normal, prevented her from developing a sense of racial subordination. She studied anthropology with Frederick Boas, concentrating on African-American folklore. *Mules and Men* (1935), is a treasury of voodoo and folklore. Zora Neale Hurston was a fashionable, lively, leading figure in the Harlem Renaissance, and her works, which often use everyday speech, engage with community 'porch life'. Her best known novel is the influential *Their Eyes Were Watching God* (1937) in which the protagonist's Nanny, points out the observed, gendered, class and race oriented balances of power against which Janey rebels:

> Honey de white man is de ruler of everything as fur as Ah been able tuh find out. Maybe it's some place way off in de ocean where de Black man is in power, but we don't know nothin' but what we see. So de white man throw down de load and tell de nigger man tuh pick it up. He pick it up because he have to, but he don't tote

it. He hand it to his womenfolks. De nigger woman is de mule uh
de world so fur as Ah can see.

(Hurston, 1986 [1937], p.29)

Janey refuses the constraints of gender, follows her third lover Teacake
and works on the land. When he dies, bitten by a rabid dog in a flood,
put out of his misery by Janey herself, she returns to tell her own tale,
and show her individuality and strength as a woman who has found
herself. The book has inspired many other African-American women,
particularly Alice Walker, who reclaimed and had republished
Hurston's work. Many of the themes and interests of her work –
community, individual women, folk culture and oral storytelling –
have been continued by those she has influenced, including Alice
Walker, Toni Morrison and Ntozake Shange.

Nella Larsen (1891–1964) is another great Harlem Renaissance writer.
Quicksand (1928) concentrates on conflicts resulting from mixed
ancestry. *Passing* (1929) looks at a middle-class African-American
woman whose colour enables her to 'pass' for white. In doing so and
marrying well, she loses her roots, friends and identity. The book
highlights the suffering caused by prejudices based on skin colour.

Maya Angelou (1928) writes about and for women of all colours and,
in particular, for otherwise ignored, silenced Black women. She finds
travel enlightening, breaking down bigotry and racism, and has
travelled widely herself, had diverse jobs and played in the first
production of *Porgy and Bess*. In her work, five volumes of
autobiography beginning with *I Know Why the Caged Bird Sings*
(1970), she uses semi-fictionalized autobiography, telling her own tale
of growing up with a strong Grandma, suffering racism from the local
dentist and poor whites. Like slave narratives before her, she uses the 'I'
figure, exploring her experiences, providing models, and she empowers
other readers who can relate to this record. Part of Maya Angelou's
analysis of racism focuses on the importance of establishing and
maintaining identity against hundreds of years of enforced adoption of
others' names, under slavery.

Ntozake Shange

i found god in myself
& i loved her/i loved her fiercely

> (Shange, 'for colored girls who have considered suicide
> when the rainbow is enuff', 1992 [1975], p.63)

Ntozake Shange (1948–) is a gifted, sensual, African-American writer of prose fiction, drama and poetry. Her acclaimed, widely performed choreopoem 'for colored girls who have considered suicide when the rainbow is enuff' (1975), was followed by her novel *Cypress, Sassafrass and Indigo* (1977) a poetic novel incorporating recipes and songs with fictional prose, looking at the development of awareness, identity and relationships, the magical and sensuous experiences of three sisters. In *Liliane* (1995) she continues to look at the imaginative and sensuous lives of Black women. It focuses on one girl concerned with communication and speaking out. Shange also concentrates on the important issue of recuperation of the past and of a woman's tradition. Her particular gift is her lyrical writing and her reclaiming of the value of the body, and of the erotic.

Alice Walker

Alice Walker (1944–), a widely read and taught Southern writer, like Toni Morrison, works to recuperate history and to give a voice to Black women whose lives have been hidden, unheard, through the establishment of sisterhood and the writing of what she terms 'womanist' prose, using quilting, the vernacular, myth and storytelling forms. Alice Walker was active in the Civil Rights Movement and taught in several colleges. Her novels include *The Third Life of Grace Copeland* (1970), *Meridian* (1976), *The Color Purple* (1983), *The Temple of My Familiar* (1989), *Possessing the Secret of Joy* (1992) and *By The Light of My Father's Smile* (1998). She also publishes short stories, essays and poems.

Alice Walker's epistolary novel *The Color Purple* is a powerful, lively and imaginative depiction of the abused life of a young Black woman, Celie, who writes to God, explaining her confused sense of guilt, shame and innocence. She is sexually abused by the man she believes to be her father, has her children stolen from her, and is married off to an abusive man, Mister. This abuse replicates the experiences of Black slaves. Celie's speaking out, initially confined to God then Nettie, is a powerful first-hand testimony. She establishes a relationship with Shug Avery, a fast bisexual fascinating nightclub singer, and finds her own identity. The novel ends with a Utopian return of Nettie and Celie's lost children, establishing harmony and the importance of identity for individuals and communities.

☀ ☀ ☀ SUMMARY ☀ ☀ ☀

- Read work by other Black women writers in the nineteenth and early twentieth centuries to see the legacy, development of focus on Black lives and energies, and different writing styles and hidden lives.

- Read more by Toni Morrison.

GLOSSARY

American Dream the idea of the American Dream derives from the pioneering frontier spirit which drove people to America hoping to seek their fortunes and their futures. It suggests that America can reward and celebrate people for their endeavours, and that it is a great, generous country. Many found that this was not the reality they actually met, encountering instead hardships, everyday difficulties and disillusionment. Many writers, including F. Scott Fitzgerald (1896–1940) who wrote *The Great Gatsby* (1925) have shown that the Dream was a deception.

Bildungsroman a story focusing on the development of an individual, their growth and change as they mature. Often nineteenth-century novels used this form to show individuals developing as members of their society, surviving various perils and evils, and growing up.

Black the use of Black as a proper noun indicates the recognition of and identification with race, with being Black. It is a seizing of identity which emerged during the Civil Rights Movement, and has been embraced particularly by Black feminists and others.

The Canon a term used to suggest the most important, most frequently read and taught literature. It includes Shakespeare and Wordsworth, but is largely a white, male middle-class group of writers. It has often excluded women and Black writers.

Colonialism Colonialism involves settlement, governing indigenous people, exploiting and developing the resources of the land, and embedding imperial government. *Colonial* literature is that produced under colonial rule, by both the settlers and the indigenous people while *colonialist* literature is that supporting colonial rule, springing from the viewpoint of the colonialists, those supporting imperialism.

Dialogic a term coined first by Russian critic Mikhail Bakhtin, dialogic suggests a dialogue, debate or argument between ideas and points of view. Typically an author might show different views of different people, or different interpretations and representations in different times and places. Together they form a debate suggesting there are no *single* right answers or interpretations – so none should be *forced* on people or events.

This aligns itself through the style of the novels, as an insight related to

Morrison's post-colonial viewpoint, i.e. that there might have been single versions of history, single sets of interpretations and value, but they have been constructed and imposed by a certain ruling group, in this instance white people over the lives of Black people.

Feminist critics Feminist critics focus on the roles of women, the representation of women (or lack of that representation) in history, culture, the arts, and issues and practices to do with women's lives. Feminist criticism considers such issues as romantic fictions, motherhood, performance, constraints by patriarchy and paternalism, and restrictions upon women's individuality and sexuality. It argues for a women-oriented language, suggesting that women, because they have had different experiences to men – i.e. have been more subordinated, less wealthy, more involved in caring for others, denied speech – are likely to favour different subject matter and to choose different language items and forms to those chosen by men.

Imperialism this is usually taken to mean literally 'of the empire'; authority assumed by a state over other states or peoples. It is often accompanied by symbolism, pageantry as well as military power.

Roman imperialism was a prime example of this, when military power and ways of life, symbols and beliefs took over from those of indigenous peoples, absorbing difference under the power of empire. Not all imperialism involves settling or colonizing.

Ku Klux Klan this was established in the American Southern States after the freeing of the slaves and still exists. Right-wing racists, they used trappings of religion and inverted them – carrying burning crosses, and used the superstitious focus of ghosts of African-Americans by dressing entirely in white with pointed hoods hiding their faces. They terrorized, lynched and murdered many Black people just because of their racial difference.

Magic realism originating in the works of Latin American writers such as Gabriel Garcia Marquez from the 1960s onwards, magic realism is a form of writing which combines both the factual or realistic, and the magical, imaginative and supernatural. Its use lets an author show both people's imaginative, lived feelings and what they could be said to actually say and do. It also enables writers to show paradox, contradictions perhaps between what people think and really experience, and what is said publicly to happen. Great twentieth-century realists include Angela Carter and Salman Rushdie.

Negritude the period of the 1930s in New York when Black people began to have their creative talents recognized and rewarded is called the 'Harlem Resistance'. One set of beliefs which developed was that of 'Negritude' which derives from the word 'negro' and defines and celebrates some specific qualities of being Black. These qualities help define people but they can also be racial stereotypes.

Other to make someone else 'Other' is to identify all that is strange and unpleasant and to blame it on someone else, to turn them into something which is not yourself, which is strange. 'Otherizing' people is an element of racism and sexism.

Post-colonial Post-colonial is a period of time, after colonialism, but it is also taken to mean in opposition to the colonial. There are numerous arguments about whether post-colonial literature can be produced during the colonial period, because of its oppositional nature, or whether, strictly speaking, it only develops once colonialism, colonial rule, has ended and independence

has been achieved. Here it will be taken to mean writing in opposition to colonialism, which has been written after colonial rule has ended, but roots prior to this ending will be mentioned. Great post-colonial critics include Edward Said and Gayatri Chakravorty Spivak.

Sharecropping when slavery was abolished in North America in 1865 many people became sharecroppers, working with the crops on a plantation for a share of those crops or the price they produced when sold. It was a hard life and a poor living.

Symbol and Metaphor these are figures of speech. A symbol is something which suggests or stands for something else, seems to define or helps the reader picture it. For example, the cross symbolizes or suggests or stands for Christianity, and water suggests or stands for life, change, movement and flow.

A metaphor is an imaginative comparison of one thing with another informing both parts of the comparison. For example, imagination could be compared to a flying bird or a growing plant, because it develops, changes and creates. Symbols tend to be widely understood and produced by cultures while metaphors are localized and in specific examples.

Chronology of Major Works

1931 Chloe Anthony Wofford born, Loraine, Ohio.

1953 Awarded a BA in English from Howard University.

1955 Awarded an MA from Cornell University, where she wrote a thesis on William Faulkner. Began her career as an instructor in English at Texas Southern University in Houston.

1957 Becomes an instructor in English at Howard University.

1958 Marries Jamaican architect Harold Morrison by whom she has two sons, Harold Ford and Slade Kevin.

1964 Divorces Harold Morrison.

1965 Begins work as a senior editor for Random House, New York.

1969 Her first novel published, *The Bluest Eye*.

1971 Becomes the Associate Professor of English at the State University of New York, Purchase.

1973 *Sula* published.

1977 *Song of Solomon* published; novel wins the National Book Critics Circle Award for fiction.

1981 *Tar Baby* published.

1984 Becomes the Albert Schweitzer Chair in the Humanities at the State University of New York, Albany.

1985 *Dreaming Emmett* (a play) published.

1987 *Beloved* published.

1988 *Beloved* wins the Pulitzer Prize for Fiction, the Robert F. Kennedy Award and the Elizabeth Cady Stanton Award from the Organization for Women.

1989 Becomes the Robert F. Goheen Professor in the Council of the Humanities and teaches fiction writing at Princeton University, New Jersey.
  Jazz and *Playing in the Dark: Whiteness and the Literary Imagination* published.
  Awarded the Nobel Prize for Literature.

1998 *Paradise* published.

2000 Co-editor with Claudia Brodsky Lacour of *Birth of a Nation'hood: Gaze, Script and Spectacle in the O.J. Simpson case.*

FURTHER READING

Books by Toni Morrison:

Morrison, Toni (1970) *The Bluest Eye*, London: Triad Grafton.

Morrison, Toni (1973) *Sula*, London: Chatto and Windus.

Morrison, Toni (1977) *Song of Solomon*, London: Triad Grafton.

Morrison, Toni (1981) *Tar Baby*, London: Triad Grafton.

Morrison, Toni (1987) *Beloved*, London: Chatto and Windus.

Morrison, Toni (1989) *Jazz*, London: Chatto and Windus.

Morrison, Toni (1989) *Playing in the Dark: Whiteness and the Literary Imagination*, Cambridge, Ma. & London: Harvard University Press.

Morrison, Toni (1998) *Paradise*, London: Chatto and Windus.

Morrison, Toni & Brodsky Lacour, Claudia (eds.) (2000) *Birth of a Nation'hood: Gaze, Script and Spectacle in the O.J. Simpson Case*, London: Vintage.

Books about Toni Morrison:

Christian, Barbara (1980) 'The Contemporary Fables of Toni Morrison' in *Black Women Novelists, the Development of a Tradition, 1892–1976*, Westport, Connecticut and London: Greenwood Press.

Christian, Barbara (1985) *Black Feminist Criticism: perspectives on Black women writers*, New York: Pergamon Press.

Evans, Mari (1985) *Black Women Writers*, London: Pluto Press.

hooks, bell (1982) *Ain't I A Woman? Black Women and Feminism*, London: Pluto Press.

Matus, Jill (1998) *Toni Morrison*, Manchester: Manchester University Press.

Peach, Linden (1995) *Toni Morrison*, London: Macmillan.

Peach, Linden (1998) *Toni Morrison; Contemporary Critical Essays*, London: Macmillan.

Smith, Barbara (1982) *But Some of Us Are Brave*, New York: Feminist Press.

Tate, Claudia (1984) *Black Women Writers at Work*, London: Oldcastle Books.

Wisker, Gina (1993) *Insights into Black Women's Writing*, London: Macmillan.

Wisker, Gina (2000) *Post Colonial & African American Women's Writing: A Critical Introduction*, London: Macmillan.

INDEX